*My Tour through
the Asylum*

Bill Dufford signs a copy of the 1961 *Beaufortonian* yearbook at the Newberry Opera House on May 11, 2015, the night he was presented with the Order of the Palmetto, South Carolina's highest civilian honor. Photograph by Ted Williams, courtesy of the Newberry Opera House.

My Tour through the Asylum

A SOUTHERN INTEGRATIONIST'S
MEMOIR

William E. Dufford

With Aïda Rogers and Salley McInerney

Foreword by Pat Conroy

12/9/'17

The struggle continues!

Bill Dufford

The University of South Carolina Press

*Publication is made possible in part by the
generous support of the William E. Dufford Fund
for Civil and Social Justice Publications.*

Published by the University of South Carolina Press
Columbia, South Carolina 29208

www.sc.edu/uscpress

Manufactured in the United States of America

26 25 24 23 22 21 20 19 18 17 10 9 8 7 6 5 4 3 2 1

Library of Congress Cataloging-in-Publication Data can be found
at http://catalog.loc.gov/.

ISBN: 978-1-61117-896-8 (cloth)
ISBN: 978-1-61117-897-5 (ebook)

This book was printed on recycled paper with 30 percent postconsumer
waste content.

"South Carolina is *too small for a republic and too large for an insane asylum.*"

James L. Petrigru to Benjamin F. Perry, December 8, 1860
From McPherson, *Drawn with the Sword*

RECORD RAINS, 2015

Jeff Greene, friend and former student of William E. Dufford

Last night, I called you to check in about the floods
and assuage my guilt at not being in touch—news
of record rains saturating your town nearly drowning me.
Your voice held the rising water at arm's length,
that calm equanimity that had once rescued me
its own force of nature.
I never learned to swim properly, thrashing
through the alien water, a spastic amid
agile amphibians. It wasn't a natural disaster,
like the flood filling your basement
with things that swim and bacterial
mud from the Saluda and the Broad.
I asked how you were and you told me
of your gratitude, reminded me that so long ago,
I had taken care of you.
When the floodwaters recede, a new world is
visible, a baptism by disaster.
Oh! I must go back to the water
now that I can swim with such grace
and know who has been saved.

Contents

❧

PART I: 1926–1968
WILLIAM E. DUFFORD

PART 2: 1969–1976

AÏDA ROGERS

Contents

PART 3: 1977–2016

WILLIAM E DUFFORD

AÏDA ROGERS AND SALLEY MCINERNEY

Illustrations

ᖰᖚ

Acknowledgments

❧

COUNTLESS THANKS go to the many former students, colleagues, and friends who lent their own recollections to this project, to Pat Conroy for his gracious foreword (first presented as an introduction at the South Carolina Governor's Awards in the Humanities induction ceremony), to Tim Conroy and Jeff Greene for their early readings of the manuscript and to Greene as well for his poem "Record Rains," to Aïda Rogers and Salley McInerney for their remarkable efforts in researching and telling a life story some ninety years in the making, and to the University of South Carolina Press and its former director, Jonathan Haupt, for preserving and sharing that story in the hopes that it might help chronicle our past and light the way to a brighter future—together, as one people.

Foreword

❦

The Summer I Met My First Great Man

PAT CONROY

IN THE SUMMER OF 1961, when I was a fifteen-year-old boy, I was lucky to have the great Bill Dufford walk into my life. I had spent my whole childhood taught by nuns and priests and there was nothing priestly about the passionate, articulate man William E. Dufford who met me in the front office of Beaufort High School dressed in a sport shirt, khaki pants, and comfortable shoes in a year that history was about to explode in the world of South Carolina education circles. Because he did not wear a white collar or carry a long rosary on his habit, I had no idea that I was meeting the principal of my new high school. In my mind, I thought as I saw him moving with ease and confidence in the principal's main office that day that he must have been a head janitor in the relaxed, unCatholic atmosphere of my first day at an American public school. It was also my first encounter with a great man.

I was a watchful boy and was in the middle of a childhood being raised by a father I didn't admire. In a desperate way, I needed the guidance of someone who could show me another way of becoming a man. It was sometime during that year when I decided I would become the kind of man that Bill Dufford was born to be. I wanted to be the type of man that a whole town could respect and honor and fall in love with—the way Beaufort did when Bill Dufford came to town to teach and shape and turn their children into the best citizens they could be.

Bill gave me a job as a groundskeeper at Beaufort High School that summer between my junior and senior years of high school. He had me moving wheelbarrows full of dirt from one end of campus to another. He had me plant grass, shrubs, trees, and he looked at every patch of bare earth as a personal insult to his part of the planet. At lunch, he took me to Harry's Restaurant every day and I watched him as he greeted the movers and shakers of that beautiful town beside the Beaufort River. He taught me, by example, how a leader conducts himself, how the principal of a high school conducts himself, as he made his way from table to table, calling everyone by their first names. He made friendliness an art form. He represented the highest ideals of what I thought a southern gentleman could be. He accepted the great regard of his fellow townsmen as though that were part of his job description. That summer, I decided to try to turn myself into a man exactly like Bill Dufford. He made me want to be a teacher, convinced me that there was no higher calling on earth and none with richer rewards and none more valuable in the making of a society I would be proud to be a part of. I wanted the people of Beaufort, or any town I lived in, to light up when they saw me coming down the street. I was one of a thousand kids who came under the influence of our magnificent principal, Bill Dufford. For him, we all tried to make the world a finer and kinder place to be.

Bill Dufford was raised in Newberry, in the apartheid South, where the civil rights movement was but a whisper gathering into the storm that would break over the South with all of its righteousness and power. Though Bill had been brought up in a segregated society, he charged to embrace the coming of freedom to southern black men and women with a passionate intensity that strikes a note of awe and wonder in me today. He went south to the University of Florida in 1966, four years after I graduated from high school, and there he came under the influence of some of the greatest educational theorists of his time. He returned to South Carolina with a fiery commitment to the integration movement in his native state. No other white voice spoke with his singular power. He headed up the school desegregation department, which sent people into all the counties in the state to help with the great social change of his time. I know of no white southerner who spoke with his eloquence about the great necessity for the peaceful integration of the schools in this state. What I had called greatness when I first saw him in high school had transfigured itself into a courage that knew no backing down, to a heroism that defied the ironclad social laws of his own privileged station from a great Newberry family.

This memoir is recognition of Bill Dufford's life well-lived in service to this state. In recent years, he has been an articulate spokesman for the diversity issue in our society. Because of Bill, his family donated their magnificent house to serve as Newberry College's alumni house. The

Dufford family has made large contributions to the Newberry Opera House, one of America's loveliest buildings. Hundreds of his students went into teaching and education because of him. I was privileged to introduce Bill Dufford when he was recognized with the South Carolina Governor's Award in the Humanities last year. Bill Dufford is one of the finest men I've ever met. It does not surprise me that we are now sharing his story in his own book; it just surprises me it took so long.

Prologue

Realizing How It Was and How It Should Have Been

SALLEY MCINERNEY

O N A SPRING DAY with the azaleas just past their Easter bloom, William E. Dufford drove his Buick sedan along Newberry's Main Street. He tapped the glass of the car window, pointing to the Ritz Theater on the left. Opened in the fall of 1936, the two-story black and white building is remarkably emblematic of his early years as a tow-headed boy called "Cotton" coming of age in the Jim Crow era of this small South Carolina community.

"Blacks could go to the Ritz, but they could not go through the front door. There was a little alley between the theater and Davis Motor Company to get to the side entrance, and then they had to sit in the balcony."

Going to the movies at the Ritz, like so many other experiences Dufford had growing up in the unassuming mill town, gave shape to his adult life as a force for change, as an educator and administrator who, with a steady hand and an equitable heart, led the way toward peaceful integration of South Carolina public schools in the 1970s.

Dufford slowed the car to a crawl, recalling how the Ritz was one of Newberry's first "air-cooled" buildings. He tapped the window again.

"The black kids, they paid the same admission price as I did, but why couldn't they sit where I sat? That wasn't fair."

As Dufford pointed out, when he came along in the 1930s and '40s, there was much that was not fair about being black in Newberry—or elsewhere throughout the South.

I

Leaving Main Street, he wound his way toward a quiet neighborhood near Newberry College. He parked the Buick in a driveway. No one would mind, he said.

Dufford stood at the corner of College and Evans Streets, taking in his surroundings. He pointed just across the way to a rambling, two-story home with a wide, wraparound porch and within spitting distance of the college campus. This is where he grew up as the baby in the family, surrounded by one brother, two sisters, a mother who took care of a big household, and a father who ran a general store.

"We didn't have any money to speak of, but we didn't know we didn't have any money. My father managed what money we did have well. My life was cloistered; it was warm and accepting."

Except for the Dufford family's cook, a black woman named Mary, Dufford said his "first memory" of African Americans in his hometown was one of "not associating with them, but viewing them from afar."

Case in point. As a twelve-year-old intrigued by the game of basketball, Dufford watched a black youth named June, who lived just one block away, playing basketball in his yard.

"I'd see June shooting basketball. He was so smooth. I was fascinated by his grace and his movement. We just looked at each other. But I never talked to him. I never played with him because he would dare not come over to my side of Cheek Street and I wouldn't dare go across to his side of the street. We lived close together, we just didn't associate together. There was a societal divide."

And a glaring physical one too.

"College Street was well-maintained. There were streetlights, sidewalks, curbs."

Dufford pointed to Lindsay Street, just one road over, where June was raised.

"This is where African American families lived. There were no curbs, no sidewalks, no streetlights. It was a vastly different environment but it was all within the city limits. The African American kids who grew up there had to walk all the way across town to get to school. I was a white kid. I had to walk about half a block to get to school. And you know, I didn't think a thing about it."

Why not?

Dufford explained, "You have to go though many of life's experiences and look back upon them. Then you realize how it was and how it should have been. You grow up. You find a broader world. That happens over the years. That doesn't happen overnight. I found my way into the broader world by going in the navy right out of high school. I began to see the world a little differently."

And he began a life dedicated to service in South Carolina public schools. After graduating from Newberry College in 1949, Dufford packed up his belongings in a blue Plymouth—it had been the family car, now it was his. He headed south to Winyah High School in Georgetown, where he was hired to teach math and physics and coach basketball, baseball, and football. He worked in a segregated school system.

But as time went on, and as public school systems throughout the South avoided integrating with "all deliberate speed," as directed in the landmark 1954 Supreme Court decision of *Brown v. the Board of Education*, pressure mounted for true integration—black students learning alongside white students in schools that housed both under one roof.

Significant change and racial unrest were brewing.

Having moved down the coast of South Carolina to be principal of Beaufort High School in the early 1960s, Dufford saw it all unfolding, on a color television set in his office.

"There were these marches going on for equal treatment and justice throughout the South. And I had the television on in my office. I saw it all. The dogs. The riot police. The fire hoses. The bombing of the churches in Birmingham. George Wallace standing in the door at the University of Alabama. Kennedy being assassinated in Dallas. It was part of my evolution from the way it was to 'That's not the way to treat people.'"

And that, Dufford said, is when he began "working to do what the law and my conscience told me we needed to do."

"If you see the world changing like we did in the early 1960s and you reflect upon your life and your experiences and do not see a need for living in the present, you're out of touch with what it's all about. You're missing a great deal of your life and what it can be and what it ought to be."

Dufford, who turned ninety years old in 2016, did not miss much—if any—of his life.

His work in school desegregation and integration in the Palmetto State drew national attention. Leaders in other states wanted to know how it was done. Dufford traveled to places like Tuscaloosa, Alabama, where race riots were raging, and he showed them.

In 2013 an annual weeklong celebration of Dufford's legacy as an educator and civil rights advocate was established at Newberry College. In 2014 he received the Governor's Award in the Humanities and then the South Carolina Order of the Palmetto.

Impressive stuff, but how would he really like to be remembered?

That's an easy one, he said. It's early afternoon. He's filled the Buick up—gas prices are better in Newberry—and he's headed south to Columbia, where he lives with a cat named Chester in a Shandon bungalow.

"I would like to be remembered as a person who had a sense of fairness."

So, another question: What gave rise to a small-town boy who began his professional career as a teacher and coach and concluded his life's work as an acclaimed, admired—yes, even adored—teacher, coach, administrator, and leader in the integration of South Carolina schools?

The query causes Dufford to pause.

"Perhaps it is a reflection of my mother and father's work. When the black sharecroppers came to the back of the general store (they couldn't come through the front door), they wanted my father to help them with what they needed. They didn't want anybody else. My mother worked with the American Legion. Those type of things seeped in. I suppose I was constantly helping those who were left out or left behind. It moved me in a different direction than many other people."

It's a direction that has impacted the lives of many, many South Carolinians.

Dufford said when he was working toward integration with students, teachers, or administrators, he used a simple, straightforward method: "I brought people in. I told them we all have a responsibility here."

"Dufford provided raw leadership," said Leighton Cubbage, who was a high school student in Sumter when Dufford arrived there in 1969, tasked with combining the town's black high school, Lincoln, and its white high school, Edmunds, into one.

"His story," Cubbage said, "is how one guy can make a difference, can make a change."

Here is that remarkable tale.

PART I

1926–1968

WILLIAM E. DUFFORD

Chapter 1

❧

The Web

FOR THE BETTER PART OF MY LIFE, I've tried to bring people together—and I mean all people. I've been a coach, a teacher, a principal, and an administrator, all in the service of public education. When people sit down and talk with me about the things I've done, they say I've had a hell of a life. But I don't think about it that way at all. It's just an ordinary life. I'm not adventurous and, except for my time in the navy, I never went too far from home here in South Carolina. I just kind of played it safe in that way. There was always too much to do here at home, and there still is. I'm ninety-one years old now, old enough to have seen my whole world change from the restrictive, insular status quo of the Jim Crow South through the civil rights movement toward a more just and equal society. But we are not there yet. *We are not there yet.* I may not see true equality, true integration of society in my lifetime, but I can tell you about the transformations I have seen, about the great people that have affected my life, and about the resistance we all encountered in trying to make life better for those around us. My life has been filled with stories, and in those memories there is the hope that others, maybe you, can see us the rest of the way.

Like I said, there have always been great people in my life—great teachers, great kids, great friends. They helped me learn that the Jim Crow South I'd grown up in wasn't right. In fact, it was crazy. For one group of people to be thought of as superior to another and to do everything they can to keep others from living a decent life—those aren't the lessons I learned in church. It took me forty years to realize I'd grown up in a cloistered world, inside a little web I couldn't get out of. When I found that bigger world of what I've come to know is just and right, I began to see things a little differently. Some of the Jim Crow stuff was not just unusual but cruel to the minority races.

That's why this book is called *A Tour through the Asylum.* When South Carolina seceded from the Union, James L. Petigru, a legislator and anti-secessionist, said this state was "too small for a republic and too large for an insane asylum." After my many years in South Carolina's public schools, I've concluded he was right.

7

Chapter 2

∾

Rambling

W HEN I WAS GROWING UP, from the time I was about twelve years old, I was known as Cotton. My hair was white, and I would ramble around town, ramble through the Newberry College campus. A student at the college would cut my hair in the dormitory. He was from Batesburg and cutting hair was how he made money and how other kids saved money. He'd sit me in a chair and wrap a sheet around my neck. Those college kids adopted me, and let me play touch football with them. They were my heroes at the time.

Another reason they might have called me Cotton was because Newberry was a mill town. There were three cotton mills then, and the children whose parents worked in them went to their own elementary schools in their mill villages. They didn't have to go to school after the fourth grade, and those who did would start fifth grade with us town kids at Speers Street Elementary School or Boundary Street Elementary School. Those mill kids went on through school with us until we graduated from Newberry High. They were good students, great kids.

But why did the decision makers, the board and culture and society at the time, think it wasn't proper to educate those kids past the fourth grade? Nobody will tell you this, but those in charge thought the kids would go work in the mill, that was the only future for them. Historically, those mill village schools were under the umbrella of the Newberry City Schools Board of Trustees.

Back then, there were two elementary schools in town and three elementary mill village schools. We didn't even count the African American schools. But when you talk about growing up in Newberry— and this is the mentality of the Jim Crow era—you don't even include the African American section over yonder. The black kids who grew up on the street behind me, they had to go across town to their school. I walked one block to get to mine. Their neighborhoods didn't have sidewalks or curbs or streetlights, and there were certain streets they knew to take if they wanted to go downtown. On our side of town, we went down College Street. Lindsay Street was the black street.

Black people knew they didn't dare come out and walk down College Street. Blacks and whites lived separate lives then. It sounds crazy to hear it now, but that's the way it was and we all just accepted it.

$\backsim$

My father loved to garden, and his garden was within view of our black neighbor's garden on the next street over. Our neighbor's name was Cat Lark and he was the college's dining room manager and main cook. He served his meals family style on white tablecloths. His wife, Florence, was the college's only maid. Between them they served Newberry College for seventy-five years, and they were still there when I was a student.

Every day after work, Daddy and Cat would call out to each other across Lindsay Street, competing for who had the best bean crop and eggplant. Daddy was the general manager at Johnson-McCracken General Store on Main Street, and he had good relationships with the black sharecroppers who came to buy their supplies on Saturday. They weren't welcome in most of the better retail stores downtown, but they would come to Johnson-McCracken in their wagons with the mules and pull up to the back door. They wouldn't go in the front door. They always wanted my daddy to serve them. Other people worked in the store too, but the African American customers would wait until "Mr. Dufford" could wait on them.

Daddy knew those customers by name and he helped them with their accounts. They couldn't go to the bank and get a loan, and they oftentimes didn't have enough to get their needs met for the next week. My daddy had a little book and on the Saturdays I worked there I would see him talking to people and writing certain things down. I don't know this for certain, but I think he was their credit union.

Because Daddy was from the country and soil was in his blood, his garden was his relaxation. I don't know if Cat Lark had soil in his blood, but he and my daddy spent a lot of time conferring across the road. I think Cat owned his home and had indoor plumbing, which would have made him different from most African Americans. Usually blacks rented from whites, and usually those houses didn't have running water. Those families had to cook and bathe as best they could, using water from a spigot outside. It seems unreal now, but again, we accepted it as the way it was then.

Here's what I think about now: I was a kid then, and I was calling Cat Lark by his first name. I never saw a black child call a white man by his first name. I knew that was wrong, that it wasn't the same level of respect for an elder. But that was the way it was. That's crazy. Crazy.

❧

The African American I had the most contact with when I was a kid was Mary, our family cook. I don't know her last name; we called her Mary Dufford. My mother had four kids in six years and she needed help, so Mary would come and take care of us and fix the meals. She and Mama would can vegetables from Daddy's garden in the kitchen together, and she cooked our food, but she didn't eat with us. She took her meals on the back porch.

We weren't rich—nobody was during the Depression—but like many white families, we could afford a cook because we didn't pay her much. At that time, cooks and maids were paid with cash without any other benefits like Social Security. We gave Mary food she could take at the end of the day too. She would pack a paper bag to take when she walked home.

I don't think Mary had a family of her own, and I just don't know what became of her. Everything changed when the war started, and we must have told her we didn't need her anymore. I hate thinking about that now. But that was part of the whole social structure of the South. We didn't pay African Americans very much in comparison to all of the work they did, which was very, very vital to our family.

Mary was smart, and she could have done a lot more than be a cook, but see, there was nothing else available for her then. Blacks were not allowed to work in the textile mills, which was the lowest form of work, but at least it was regular. The only thing you could do was be a maid if you were female or repair the tires at a filling station if you were male. Or you could stay out in the country and do your farming and live on a little farm. Of course, you probably didn't own the land and were share-cropping, which is, again, a system of servitude.

I remember that Mary lived on Cornelia Street, in a little house that seemed to be attached to another house. As white people would say about the black people who worked for them, "She was family." But then, she just couldn't live with us.

❧

There was an intelligent black community in Newberry when I was growing up, but we didn't know that. Maceo Nance, later the president of South Carolina State University, grew up in Newberry. Frances Davenport Finney, a teacher who married Ernest Finney Jr., South Carolina's first black Supreme Court justice, grew up in Newberry. Living behind us, on the corner of Lindsay and Cheek Streets, was Dr. Julian Grant. He was a black doctor from Bennettsville who went to Meharry Medical College in Nashville. Black folks at that time were making great sacrifices to come back and teach and be doctors, dentists. I don't know if there ever was a black dentist in Newberry, but Dr. Grant came back to serve his own people. He couldn't admit his patients to the Newberry hospital, so he built his own clinic, People's Hospital, on Vincent Street, in 1937. He was Newberry's first African American doctor.

Of course, that's not what interested me then. I would watch one of his sons play basketball. The Grants had a goal in their yard, and the son they called June could really play. He was about my age. Even in the 1930s, he had a goal. Even in the 1930s, he had a shot.

White boys didn't play basketball back then. Like many southern towns, Newberry had football and baseball. We knew about basketball because of the textile teams playing it in other parts of the state. We had no idea how to play the game, or even how to handle the ball.

Anyway, it wasn't like I could ask June to show me how to play. He lived on Lindsay Street, and white kids weren't supposed to go over there.

Chapter 3

Good Home Training

L IKE ALL GOOD CHILDREN of the Jim Crow South, I was carefully taught by our society to uphold a time-honored status quo. To honor Confederate Memorial Day each spring, fifth graders at Speers Street and Boundary Elementary Schools marched to the Newberry Confederate Memorial. We'd all wear white, sing "Dixie" and "The

Bonnie Blue Flag," and wave little Confederate flags. Like most kids, we didn't know what we were doing.

By that time, 1936, my parents had bought our house on College Street. It was big—six thousand square feet—and tremendously run-down. I was ten by then, and our family of six had long outgrown the small rental home one block up College Street. My parents were very frugal. Not stingy. My daddy knew how to manage money, and he knew the only way we could afford our new house was by renting out an apartment within it to respectable couples, which would help pay the mortgage.

My parents were smart people. They didn't have much formal education—I don't think either of them finished high school—but they knew education was important. There was no question in their minds that their kids would be going to college, and there was no question it would be Newberry College. It's a Lutheran school, and my father's people had been Lutheran ministers, starting with my great-grandfather, Ephraim Dufford, who came to the South Carolina seminary in Lexington from Butler County, Pennsylvania, in 1848. We belonged to the Lutheran Church of the Redeemer, and my parents were very active in it. Our whole family went every Sunday, except for when Mama stayed home to make dinner.

Both my parents had very tough upbringings, and I think when they moved to Newberry they finally found a place they could settle in and feel safe, raise a family, and call home. It's interesting to think they could provide such a stable upbringing for us, because they never had one themselves, and many of my mother's sisters and brothers were unable to achieve stable lives as adults. They sometimes would have to come and live with us. Everyone was poor during the Depression, but there was rarely a need that couldn't be met.

My father's full name was Cornelius Adolphus Dufford, but everybody called him "Neal." He was born in Lone Star, in Calhoun County, in 1897. His mother died in childbirth when he was three, and he had six older siblings. Then his father died before Daddy was eight. It was not an easy life, because he was in a poor, rural part of the state right at the turn of the century. I don't know who was responsible for getting clothes on the back of this kid or feeding him or making sure he went to school. He did some schooling somewhere, no question, because he had great handwriting.

Daddy never talked about his childhood. My sister Virginia did some family research and learned Daddy lived with a cousin and then a sister before joining the South Carolina National Guard. He served his country when Mexico tried to regain Texas and later in France during World War I. He kept a journal of those days, which is now at USC's Caroliniana Library. When World War II started twenty years later, he wanted to join the service again. But my mother said, "No, you have two sons who are going to serve," and we did.

My mother was Alma Cole, and she met my daddy in Kingstree. He was working at a furniture store after getting his honorable discharge from the army, and she was working at a drugstore. I'm not sure where all she lived before she got to Kingstree, but I know she was born in Halifax County, Virginia, where her mother was from. Her mother was Laura Brown Cole, and she was a character. She was the only grandparent I knew. Her husband died in 1912, leaving her with five daughters and one son. My mother was somewhere in the middle of those kids. Having no occupational skills, Laura and her children moved from Virginia to Guilford, North Carolina, where she became something like a housemother at a children's home. It was a way for her to keep her kids fed and in school. I think that children's home may now be part of the Elon University campus.

My grandmother was a romantic, so if a nice-looking man came down the line, she could arrange something. A traveling piano tuner came to tune the piano at the orphanage, so she went with him, taking the kids and moving around. They had a son, and somehow they ended up in Kingstree. By the time my parents met in 1919, most of the rest of my mother's family had moved to Atlanta. So my parents married in Atlanta in 1920. The four of us kids came quickly: my brother, C. A., named for my father, in 1921, then my sisters, Virginia and Doris, in 1923 and 1925. I'm the youngest, born in 1926.

I'm not sure how my parents got to Newberry. I just know they came in 1923 and put down their roots. My father ran for city council and served twenty-some years. When World War II started, he was appointed to the Selective Service Board and became a neighborhood warden, walking the streets at night to make sure nobody's lights could be seen. People on the East Coast were fearful of submarines and shellings, so even though we were far inland, we were told to cover our windows to make sure the outside was dark. It was a time when everybody pulled together to make sure our country was safe from harm.

Both of my parents were active in the American Legion. My father was the commander of Post 24 and a district commander, and in 1948 my mother was elected president of the South Carolina American

Legion Auxiliary. You have to have a mission statement as the president and, this is very unusual in 1948, my mother's mission was to support UNICEF, the United Nations International Children's Emergency Fund. The United Nations had just been formed in '45, so this was brand new. That means she was forward-looking, she understood the world is not just Newberry or South Carolina or the United States. There's a bigger world she was concerned about. She knew even then that we need to be concerned about infants, kids, and education, wherever they might be. That's a hell of a time for anyone to be thinking globally about things like that.

By 1948, when she was president, I was the only child left at home. So I helped her with her speeches. She and a good friend of hers, Grace Dennis, who was also active in the American Legion, would drive around the state talking to different auxiliary groups.

My parents were relatively quiet, but they got involved in things of interest to them and that dealt generally with the betterment of the local community, state community, and national community, whatever it was. And they were great with people. They were really motivated to do the things that needed to be done, and that motivated me.

Chapter 4

$\backsim$

One of the Boys

MAYBE because my parents were good with people is why I like being around people myself. I don't need to be the leader; I just want to be a part of the group. At my first job after college, in Georgetown, I had a ninth-grade homeroom class that was mostly girls. One morning most of those girls who were in the chorus started singing, and I sang with them. Then every morning after roll call, we'd sing. We didn't do all this hollering; we harmonized.

I didn't need to do a solo, just to sing together. But when those girls were juniors, they invited me to sing at their junior-senior. I was the entertainment. I sang "Down Among the Sheltering Palms" and I was scared to death. I wore a dinner jacket and white tie, and the chorus teacher, Miss King, accompanied me on the piano. That was an unforgettable moment in the Winyah High gym.

I was like that growing up too. Part of the group. Willing to go along. I would chase footballs for the Newberry College football team, and when I was about twelve I became the baseball team's batboy for home games. They invited me on their spring practice trip to Florida, where they'd play the baseball teams at Rollins College, Stetson University, and the University of Miami. Billy Laval was Newberry's coach then. He didn't invite me, the players did, and they took care of me. Wherever the team ate, I ate. Wherever the team stayed, I stayed. I was the batboy; I was working for them.

My parents had no problems with me going. There was a great sense of trust back then. Coach Laval would sit behind the bus driver, and I would sit on the front row. I called him "Coach," and the players called him "Old Man." He was nearing the end of his coaching career then, but he was still at Newberry when I was a student. He'd had a remarkable career earlier, at the University of South Carolina and Furman. Coach Laval holds the all-time win-loss percentage record at USC in football, basketball, and baseball.

Florida wasn't much in the late 1930s, except for oranges. There were beaches, but they weren't developed as they are now. We didn't hit the beaches at all. One thing going on in Florida was jai alai, where you could gamble. I was too young to go, so the players would take me to the movie and they would go play.

At night we would slip out of the motels and into the orange groves. We'd take pillowcases from the motel and fill them up with oranges. One time when it was dark we told the bus driver—he was a student too—to pick us up at certain time. We were sneaking around orange groves, and then we ran into the middle of a grove—and there was the owner's house. Talk about scrambling! We had a little problem meeting the bus, because we'd separated at that time. It was great little adventure and we didn't think we were doing anything illegal. Those escapades were never mentioned by Coach Laval or in his presence, but he probably knew more than he let on. That was his nature.

The trips to Florida stopped when World War II came. Coach Laval had a hard time cultivating teams because so many students left to serve. I was in ninth grade when Japan attacked Pearl Harbor, and that took our high school coach, Henry Hedgepath, into the service. He was probably in his early forties, but if you could breathe, they wanted you to serve. So for my last two and a half years in high school we had no coach or interscholastic sports. Gas was rationed, rubber for tires was scarce, and even if we had a coach and a team, there was no way to travel to play other schools. That was very disappointing. It changed the whole complexion of life, probably for the better.

Instead, we played on intramural teams. We would play against each other in physical education class. Mr. A. P. Boozer was the boys' P.E. teacher, and for some reason I would end up being the coach in those P.E. classes. I didn't apply for the job. Maybe because I'd been the Newberry batboy, the other kids associated me with sports.

But let me tell you what was good about those intramural teams: they gave everybody an opportunity to play. Kids who weren't as gifted athletically could play, and so could kids who lived out in the country and otherwise would have to go home before after-school practice. It brought people closer and we got to know each other better. It was one of my first lessons in what good can come from a sense of equal inclusion in an activity.

I think about how many town kids looked down on the mill kids when we were younger. Through these intramural sports we learned that they were really great kids. We probably would have learned that there were really great African American kids in Newberry too. But it would have been inconceivable for us to play with them. The school boards back then were run exclusively by white men, and the black schools fell under their jurisdiction. The boards were following the law that separate was equal. But they didn't think blacks were equal. To them, African Americans didn't have enough sense to have their own trustees. That was the mentality and the sadness of it then.

$\sim$

Newberry did some good things for the kids during the war, at least for the white kids. One thing the town did was rope off Chapman Street, right in front of my house, on Saturday mornings and maybe Wednesday afternoons so kids would have a place to roller-skate. The strangest thing is, I never learned to roller-skate. I could never get the courage or the sense of balance, so I quit trying. My sisters, they loved to skate. Naturally, there was no place for black children to roller-skate. The town's recreation department wouldn't have planned anything like that for them.

Back then Newberry had two movie theaters, the Ritz and the Wells, and they were both on Main Street. African Americans had their own private entrances. I don't remember seeing a black person go in a movie. The Ritz had a separate ticket booth for blacks on the side.

There was also the Newberry Drive-In, about two miles north of town, and by law blacks were not allowed to go. Few would have had cars anyway. Blacks could work for you, they could cook for you and care for your little children, but they weren't allowed to go to the movies and sit with you. The thinking was businesses could make money off of them, but they were not going to treat them fairly. Things were either black or white. I didn't go to the drive-in either, but that was because we didn't have a car.

What interested me more than skating or movies was basketball. Mr. Ellis Stockman, our science teacher at Newberry Junior High, started a team right before the war started. That was my chance to learn how to do what I'd seen June Grant doing earlier. We'd play in the junior high school gym after school. It was small, not regulation size.

None of us knew much about basketball. I think we just played one another. I don't remember there being uniforms. I know there was no dressing room. You had to come ready to play.

Mr. Stockman was our coach. He was young, and I think he was interested in it. He didn't have to start a team. This was something he did through the love of teaching. He later became the superintendent of schools in Batesburg-Leesville.

I liked all my teachers, all the ones I ever had. I could probably name them all even now. I tended to identify with them as I came to like them, and I think that must be a good connection for a student to make with a teacher or with a mentor of any kind. It inspired me to want to be more like the good teachers in my own schooling. It seemed natural to me, for example, that I would start basketball clinics for the kids in Georgetown when I got there a few years later, following the good model of Mr. Stockman.

My experience with teachers began early. My parents rented our first home on College Street from Professor Edwin B. Setzler. He was an English professor at Newberry College and an expert on syntax. For a mill town, Newberry was pretty rural, and Dr. Setzler would walk to his barn through our yard to milk his cow and then go back to campus. Cats are always drawn to barns and pastures, and I made friends with those cats. I adopted them.

My sisters made fun of me, but in the summer I'd run around without a shirt on, and my cat would ride on my shoulders. We'd climb trees that way, and they never scratched me.

Professor Setzler's wife was Una Lake Setzler, and she was the principal at Newberry Junior High. She was also an English teacher and big into grammar. Back then you diagramed sentences. One day after school she asked me to come into her classroom; she wanted my opinion on whether a word was an adjective or adverb. That was impressive that she asked me as a thirteen- or fourteen-year-old kid. She might not have really needed my opinion, but it made me feel good to be asked. I hadn't thought about this, but maybe that's why I always tried to ask my students what they thought about things, to engage them in that same way.

❧

My life in Newberry as a young boy was very contained. I could walk to the college behind the house, I could walk to the high school three blocks away, and I could walk across Chapman Street to the elementary school. Uncle Will and Aunt Julia Wicker—they weren't really our relatives, but everybody called them that—lived in a two-story house across from us. Behind their home they had a small country store. Uncle Will got killed in the early 1930s in an automobile accident. Aunt Julia had a pronounced limp, and her livelihood was running that store. She needed someone to tend the store when she went to the bathroom in the big house, so if I was out and about, she'd call me over to mind it. I'd sell ice cream and sodas and loaves of bread. You could get a cigarette for a penny; a pack was twenty cents. Aunt Julia would sell them five for a nickel. She had canned goods, pork and beans, and sardines. In the back of the store, the college students would play cards.

Outside Aunt Julia's, the students had a great game of ringers. It's kind of like horseshoes but you'd use washers. You'd get a team and try to throw the washers in a cup eighteen feet away. You'd get a point for being close and five if you got a ringer. We didn't have room for horseshoes, so we developed this game using washers. It was a great sport, and very popular at Newberry College in the 1930s and '40s.

At the time, girls didn't go to Aunt Julia's. They couldn't leave campus without getting permission from the dean of women. She needed to know where they were going and how long they were going to be gone.

While I can still remember it clearly, my whole life in Newberry is gone now. Aunt Julia's and my first house on College Street are gone. The pasture and barn where I played is now part of Newberry College, and the students play soccer and softball there now. That's how the world looks when you get to be my age. You can look almost anywhere and see what was and what is. The challenge is to see the lessons in those changes—and to see what might yet be.

Chapter 5

༄

Separation at the Pool, Unity on the Home Front

ONE OF THE BIGGEST THINGS that's gone in Newberry is the swimming pool at Margaret Hunter Park. I was a lifeguard there in high school. I didn't save any lives, unless you count teaching kids how to swim as saving lives. My own swimming lessons came from the Red Cross; I still have my badge from 1941. On Saturdays I helped my daddy at the Johnson-McCracken store, making about $2.50 a day— naturally, in cash. But during the week in the summer I worked at the Margaret Hunter Park pool. I don't remember getting a paycheck, but I could swim for free and I liked that.

The WPA built the pool for the city in 1935, and the park itself had been a project of the Newberry Civic League. It had all kinds of trees, shrubbery, and a little bridge over the stream running through the park. My mother was in the Civic League; that was a group of ladies who championed ways to make the community better. They didn't have any money to do it themselves. There was really no place nearby to swim— if you had a car you could drive twenty miles to Lake Murray—so for most of us, the pool was great.

Of course, if you belonged to Newberry's upper class, you could go to the Newberry Country Club and swim in the natural pool. There was a golf course there too. My parents didn't belong to the club and the mill families didn't. But the mill owners and mill managers, and the people who owned stores downtown, they were all members.

I liked lifeguarding because it gave me something to do and I got to have a lot of people around me. I'd rather do that than read a book in the library. Lifeguarding gave me a solid introduction to kids from the textile mills too. Even though I'd gone to school with them starting in fifth grade, I didn't get a chance to know them as well as I did at the pool. Schools didn't have lunch then, so kids didn't have a chance for much personal interaction.

Mainly kids came to the pool, and there was a shallow wading pool on one end. You had to pay a dime to get in. African Americans wouldn't *dare* show up at the pool. They never protested that at the time, however. I think I knew they knew that the swimming pool was for white folks. It wasn't right, it just *was*.

The only exception was the black maids of white families. They would bring the little white children to the wading pool and sit in a little section apart from the rest. They were motherly women, very quiet, very respectful, even respectful to kids like me. They called me mister. I might have said "yes, ma'am," I don't know. But I didn't know their names.

In the 1950s, word got out that a black person had attempted to go in the pool. Soon after, the pool was filled with dirt and that was the end of it. Can you imagine now a time when a small town would rather have no swimming pool at all than one shared by people of different races?

∽

Like everybody else in my generation, I remember the attack on Pearl Harbor. We'd been to church, eaten our Sunday dinner, and the whole family was in the sitting room when we heard a big outburst of hollering. It was the boys at Newberry College who'd just heard about the attack. They knew they'd be called up to serve. We turned on the radio to find out what was going on.

The next day was normal; I had just turned fifteen and was in the ninth grade. At school people knew we'd been attacked. Most of us didn't know where Pearl Harbor was. We knew we had a naval base there, but there were no pictures because we didn't have television. We're being told verbally there are some ships that have been sunk, but nothing hits you more than the visual image. You can talk about ships being sunk in the Pacific, but you don't get the full picture until you see the scrambling, the destruction, the loss of life.

We were looking to our president, whom everybody adored, to find out what he was going to do. On the morning of December 8, FDR spoke on the radio. It was his famous speech, where he said December 7 will be a day that lives in infamy. War had been declared that day. We found that out when we came home from school. Public schools didn't serve lunch then; parents kept meals for kids when they got home at two. In fact, it was because of the draft in that war that the nation first learned that kids from the South were undernourished and underweight. FDR came in with federal lunch programs as a result. The government also discovered students from the South weren't as well educated, and it began to require that the twelfth grade be added before students could graduate high school. (My classmates and I finished after eleventh grade.) FDR did so many good things for this country and was an inspirational leader in a time of crisis and war.

Except for the shutdown of interscholastic athletics and the Newberry baseball team's trips to Florida, the war didn't have a profound effect on me personally. When things became worse, we had to devote our raw materials to the war effort. That's when I first saw margarine. Before, you had butter. Margarine used to come in a big, white, one-pound package. It looked like lard, and on the side you had some yellow powder that you added to give it coloring. I didn't know the difference between butter and margarine. We were lucky to have plenty of vegetables, fresh and canned, thanks to my daddy's garden. We had chickens too.

But it was a different time. People put flags in their homes and yards, and there was an attitude and atmosphere where everybody became a little more committed to a sense of America. In my family, we already had that sense because my father fought in World War I and my parents were involved in the American Legion. During World War II they became even more active in the Legion. Along with his duties as a neighborhood night warden, my father was a member of Newberry County's Selective Service Board, which made sure men signed up for service and evaluated those who could be exempted.

During the day, kids played pickup football and baseball at the park near Speers Street Elementary School. Because the town had to be dark at night, we stayed at home and listened to the radio. So our age group didn't really have the opportunity to learn how to date, but the unity of purpose during the war brought people together in a way we wouldn't have been brought together otherwise.

I don't feel cheated, though I'm sure we missed out on much that was more common in the lives of later generations of teenagers. It was different. And I kept lifeguarding until after I graduated from high school.

Chapter 6

❦

Heeding the Call

M Y BROTHER, C. A., was a senior at Newberry College when the war started. He had been accepted to medical school in Charleston and planned to join the army. The U.S. military needed doctors, and we knew they would let him continue his studies. I finished Newberry High School on June 6, 1944, D-day, when the Allied troops landed on the beaches in Normandy. On June 7, I started college at Newberry. I was seventeen, too young to join the service. But I knew that when I turned eighteen I'd have to serve my country.

I chose the navy, not because I had any great love for the ocean or even a need to see the world from a ship. I based my decision on my own personal comfort. I figured being on a ship was cleaner than being in the army, where you'd be stuck in the trenches, and I also figured the food would be better. So, in November 1944, with one semester's credit from Newberry College, I left home on a bus from the Wiseman Hotel.

At the naval base in Charleston I was processed and sent to Bainbridge, Maryland, for basic training. That lasted ninety days. It was my first Thanksgiving and Christmas away from home. It was also my first time with people from other places, and it was a great experience.

My biggest lesson from basic training was learning how to shoot a rifle. Here's the wisdom of someone unaccustomed to using firearms: I thought I'd move that rifle butt away from my shoulder. The instructor said "strap it tight." When the instructor moved away, I thought, "I'm not doing that." Well, I went in that night and my arm from my elbow to my neck was black and blue. I nearly killed myself with my wisdom about guns. I'm still not sure how I passed that test.

Once, during boot camp, the petty officer in charge of training sailors disciplined me for grinning in formation. I had to run laps holding my rifle above my head. Basic training didn't kill me. It was a great experience. It gave me a sense of bonding with people from different sections of the country, although I wasn't fully aware of that valuable experience at the time.

I never had chow duty or latrine duty in the navy. My detail was feeding coal into the furnace. I already had experience at that; as a kid, my chore was bringing in coal and wood. I had to stoke the furnace every two hours in four-hour shifts. I learned the navy runs on four-hour shifts. As a result, boot camp teaches punctuality and discipline.

I left basic training as a seaman second class. The skills tests I'd taken showed I had the aptitude for a new science the British developed in 1942. I was assigned to the Radio Detection And Range, or RADAR, school. We trained in Newport, Cape Cod, Brigantine Island, New Jersey, and Virginia Beach, learning how to track planes and ships and get their speeds, directions, and distances. We had to know trigonometry and how angles came together. I'd always been pretty good in math and science, and that skills test showed I'd be well suited for radar.

What we didn't know was that we were part of a crew forming for a new cruiser, the USS *Los Angeles*. I was one of about sixty seamen learning to operate the radar air search and surface search machines and to work in the Combat Information Center. We didn't know why we were learning what we were learning or doing what we were doing; we were just taking orders. When we got to Virginia Beach we were funneled into a cadre, to be the radar division for the ship.

Most of my shipmates were from the North, but there were a few southerners in our group. I was the only one from South Carolina. We would have discussions, as ignorant seventeen- and eighteen-year-olds do, about the Civil War. The northern boys would jokingly say, "We were just trying to teach you how to treat people." And I'd say, "You must have liked us because you fought hard to get us back." We didn't have fights, though, and they were great kids.

In Virginia Beach we took over the Cavalier Hotel and trained in Little Creek, about a half-hour away. Our reveille was Charlie Barnet and his orchestra playing "Cherokee."

That's where we were when FDR died. We stood at the train tracks when his body went back to Washington from Warm Springs. I remember how slow that train moved, and how sad it was, and how people were dressed in their best clothes, watching it. The nation lost a great man. Even as a young man, I understood that.

Chapter 7

❦

Out in the World

WHEN THE USS *Los Angeles* was commissioned in Philadelphia in 1945, the boys in our radar division were on the ship. My parents came, and C. A. too. We didn't know a thing about the ship and we were supposed to show our parents around; I almost didn't know the fantail from the bow or the port or starboard. We had never been on a ship.

It was a big day for us and the citizens of Los Angeles and the U.S. Navy. This cruiser was top of the line and had brand-new equipment, and we were specially trained. The whole thing was unique.

The ship's contractor was the Philadelphia Naval Yard. Corporate America would build ships for the U.S. military. Cities would raise money to have cruisers named for them. The mayor of L.A. was there, as was the commanding officer, Captain J. A. Snackenberg. It was very formal. The band played and the chaplain prayed for the ship and crew and the mayor said how proud the people of Los Angeles were to have a ship named in honor of their city.

Then the ship was taken on "shakedown," a cruise to make sure everything worked as it should. We went to Guantanamo Bay, where the navy was headquartered, by way of Norfolk to pick up ammunition that had been stored in the mountains of West Virginia. There were fifteen hundred crew members on the *Los Angeles*, and for many of us this was our first time on a ship. So for us, the radar team, it was the first time working with moving targets and making sure things were functioning. The most exciting thing that happened on shakedown was when the tug commander cussed at Fire Control for firing at the tug instead of the target they were towing!

We never went to shore once we got to Guantanamo Bay. We stayed about a month and then went back to Norfolk to replenish our supplies, and then through the Panama Canal to Los Angeles. We came into Long Beach Harbor at the same time several other ships returned from fighting in the Pacific. Those ships and sailors were beat up bad and were going to the docks for repair; they'd been in battle for months. We were brand-new and had never been to war. Who do you think was greeted, us or them? The mayor and citizens came out for us. There was a band and all this ceremony again. It was the first time Los Angeles had a ship named for them. The sailors who'd been fighting for a year were understandably upset by this. They'd been in combat and we were the ones getting the fanfare homecoming. I can imagine them thinking, "What in the hell is this?"

We spent three weeks in the Los Angeles harbor. For a boy from little old Newberry, several things happened that left me feeling a bit more exposed to the big, wide world. I saw some CBS studio shows and was promoted to seaman first class. I also went to a collegiate football game—Southern Cal against Pepperdine University—at Los Angeles Coliseum. That was a new experience for me. I had never seen a football game in a stadium like that. I was really in the big city!

Then we sailed to Pearl Harbor. We spent Christmas there. Then we left for Shanghai, to take over from the USS *Fall River*. Our mission was to patrol the China coast, particularly between Shanghai and Hong Kong on the South China Sea. There was very little danger. The closest we got to combat was some rumbling in Peking, where the communists were fighting the nationalists north of us. We had a company of Marines on the cruiser, and they were expected to go on shore into battle. Our ship was going top speed, thirty to forty knots, or forty miles per hour, to Tsingtao, and we could hear the guns over the hills when we got there. Us little eighteen- and nineteen-year-olds, we weren't looking forward to battle. All the officers got out their charts and were plotting, but we didn't want to go to war. And it turned out we didn't have to.

We spent six to eight months in Shanghai. It was still kind of torn up from the Japanese invasion in the 1930s. But we'd have a good time on shore leave in Hong Kong. We'd be there just overnight, or a weekend at most, and go downtown on trolleys and eat in good restaurants. Our ship formed a basketball team, and our radar company was the K-1 division. We'd play touch football on a recreation field, and basketball at the Hong Kong YMCA. The ship had a mimeographed newspaper, *The Angelean*, and I was the sports editor.

Ships were busy places and there wasn't much opportunity to get to know people who weren't in your division. The only chance to meet other guys was during meals. I did find out there was another kid from Newberry County on the *Los Angeles*, Harold Pitts. He was a cook, and now he's a successful farmer back in Newberry County.

The harbors were different in Shanghai and Hong Kong. In Hong Kong, you had to tie to a buoy out in the harbor and take a small boat to shore. In Shanghai, you could dock in the Yangtze River. The people of Shanghai had just been through war; they'd been fighting the Japanese for years. The poor Chinese would propel their sampans in the Yangtze River and come up beside us for the food thrown overboard our ship. Seeing the bombed USS *Arizona* in Pearl Harbor was difficult for us. But seeing bodies of the poor floating down the Yangtze River in Shanghai—that was stark.

∾

By 1945 we all knew the war was winding down and that we would win. A lot of the petty officers were being discharged, so I was promoted to Watch, Quarter, and Station Officer. That meant I was in charge of scheduling watch for sixty people, as well as assigning cleaning stations and general quarters stations. Shifts were for four hours, and I'd assign my own cleaning station. I was gracious: I took a small room with nothing to clean, folded one of my navy caps under my head, and napped. I needed to get away for a little bit. If you had watch, you weren't assigned to a cleaning station. I didn't see it as a big job, but as I reflect on it, that was pretty tough for a little nineteen-year-old from South Carolina who wasn't going to continue on toward a career in the navy. I also was the "captain's talker." We were four decks down getting information from the Combat Information Center (CIC). I had to convey that information to Captain Snackenberg several levels up on the ship's bridge through a sound-powered phone system. I don't know why that job came to me with my good old southern accent, but it did.

I was in Shanghai when I got my discharge notice. I picked up an old troop carrier, the USS *Breckinridge*, with sailors from all over the Pacific and came back to San Diego, the major West Coast separation port. I took a train back to South Carolina that summer with other kids from the East Coast. The train was coal-fired. With no air-conditioning, we sat in those cars with the windows down and smoke blowing in as we traveled through Arizona, New Mexico, Texas. It was not something I really want to remember, but it's something I can't forget. Back in Charleston, I was honorably discharged in August 1946.

I thought about staying in the navy. I think I could have adjusted to a career in the service and gone up the line. I did feel a great loss of the people I'd been associated with, particularly the radar division. There had been opportunities for bonding in different locations with different people. It was a great thing to live with people who come from different places and learn they aren't really that different from you, they're just like

26

the rest of us. It was later before I knew the same was true of African Americans. The only blacks aboard the *Los Angeles* were stewards who served the officers. They wore different uniforms and took their meals separately from the rest of us.

Still, dealing with people in close proximity from different sections of the country helped me understand humanity and human beings. Plus, the food was pretty decent, it really was. I'd been right about that when I chose the navy over the army.

Chapter 8

❦

From Navy Veteran to Frat Boy

THERE WAS NO QUESTION I'd be coming back to Newberry. I looked forward to it. And soon I was back in the regular swing of things, which means slow compared to today. But still, things were different. I was the last child living at home—Virginia was working on her master's degree at the University of Colorado and Doris had married and moved to Florida. C. A. was in the Philippines, doing his medical internship with the army. He came back home in 1950 and was Newberry's first— and only—pediatrician.

Things were different at Newberry College too. The G. I. Bill meant kids who probably wouldn't have gone to college got a chance to go, and there were plenty of older students on campus too—many of them with wives and children. Former military barracks were erected for science labs and housing for married students. The whole atmosphere was different than when I'd left. I used the G. I. Bill as well. Except for the summer school session and semester before I left for the navy, I didn't spend a cent for my undergraduate education.

Having experienced the dormitory lifestyle in the navy, I stayed at home, where the price was right and the food was good. My father still had his garden, and his vegetables tasted as good as ever. But the navy had introduced me to different places and people, and Newberry College in 1946 did the same.

If you looked at the Newberry yearbook for the year I graduated, you would think I was more than I was. Somehow I got elected president of the student body and president of the Newberry Day Students Club, which was huge then because of all the local kids who could now afford to go to college. About 50 percent of the student body was made up of day students, and those kids knew who I was, so I had a built-in block of guaranteed votes. But I don't remember making a speech or asking somebody to vote for me. I always felt somebody nominated me and there was nobody else to run. I would fall into leadership roles like this.

My senior year, I was selected for national recognition in *Who's Who among Students in American Universities and Colleges*, and on campus I received the Cromer Citizenship Award, which was given by the faculty. And I was president of my fraternity, Phi Tau. Newberry College had two fraternities then, neither of them nationally affiliated. I also was editor of the yearbook and co-captain of the basketball team—and let me tell you, I wasn't a good player.

Coach Laval was still there, and he was more of a baseball and football coach than basketball. When it came to college sports, Newberry was like the rest of South Carolina—football was all-important.

The professors I lived in awe of as a kid were now my instructors. My math professor, Wilmer Gaver, was a great teacher. One time when I was about fifteen or sixteen, cutting grass with a push mower, he hid behind a tree and then jumped out and scared me. But you couldn't get out of his class without knowing math.

Majoring in education was different than it is today. There was no practice teaching, no practical experience. Everything was theoretical and out of the textbook. You'd talk about it and then move on to the next thing. I think that's the way it was at all colleges then.

The thing Newberry College helped most with was interaction and personal types of things rather than subject-focused education. How to deal with people—that's not in the textbook, but that's what I learned.

Other things weren't in the textbooks either. We didn't have a good background in or understanding of history, and our social studies courses were incomplete. American history and the Civil War were discussed in college history classes, but not the sociological impact of the war. We never talked about slavery, Reconstruction, and what it had meant to different races and how it affected different races. It was not discussed, not in the textbook, but I don't hold that against Newberry as an institution. If you don't talk about something, it doesn't exist. If you don't hear about it, it doesn't exist. Slavery and the condition of people who were different from us weren't part of our learning experience.

It might not have been said directly, but the way it came across in college levels, you got the idea the South was right. We never talked about the other side of the issue, or the significance about how people treated others. We were taught about states' rights, and that each state should have the right to do what it wants to do. Slavery was never mentioned, or seldom mentioned.

The only things we talked about were the glory of battle, how heroically the southern troops fought, all the hardships they went through, and the land that was taken away from the southern plantation owners. We didn't talk about those plantation owners who were using African Americans in very inhumane ways to make money for themselves so they could live the great lifestyle. To the southern way of thinking—and later the southern way of teaching—land was taken from the plantation owners, who were looking out for the "darkies."

When I became a high school principal in Beaufort, the first school I saw as I drove into town was Robert Smalls High School, the African American school then. As an educated man, I should have known who Robert Smalls was, but I didn't. A Beaufort native, Smalls was an enslaved boat pilot in Charleston who took over a Confederate ship and piloted it to the Union lines and to freedom for his family and crew. After the Civil War he served as a U.S. Congressman and championed equal access to public education for blacks and whites. That's the kind of history we missed when I was growing up.

When I was at Newberry High School, the custodian was a white man. But at Newberry College the custodians and cooks were all black, and the maids and cooks all wore white aprons. Cat Lark was still cooking and his wife, Florence, was still cleaning when I was there. I didn't think anything about it. Even though the navy took me around the world, I still only associated with white people.

"He Knew How to Teach"

Dutchin Hardin was a fourteen-year-old ninth grader at Winyah High School when Bill Dufford came to Georgetown. Dufford was tall, handsome, and twenty-three years old. In 1949 Georgetown, young teachers were unusual, and it wasn't long before his students—and colleagues—came to adore him.

"All the girls had crushes on him," Hardin recalled. "The boys gave him a hard time. They loved him, but they would tease him."

Hardin was in Dufford's homeroom class, where she and her freshmen classmates sang in the mornings. Three years later, they asked their teacher to sing at their junior-senior prom. Dufford's performance of "Down Among the Sheltering Palms" in the decorated Winyah High gym "was a real treat" for her and others.

As a teacher, though, Dufford was all business. He taught Hardin algebra. "He was a good teacher, and when I say good, he knew how to teach. A lot of teachers don't know how."

Hardin would teach under Dufford for six years in Beaufort, struggling to call her former teacher "Bill" and not "Mr. Dufford." He'd become principal at Winyah Junior High when she left for Winthrop in 1953—the year the high school annual was dedicated to him.

Then Dufford left Georgetown for Beaufort in 1958. "One of the older teachers told me years later that everybody cried when Bill left," Hardin said. "They hated for him to leave."

Chapter 9

༄

Winyah Gators

I THINK MY MOTHER wanted me to be a dentist, but I couldn't see working in somebody's mouth for the rest of my life. I liked the teachers and coaches I knew as a kid, and my family was okay when I said I was going into education. Being a teacher is a noble profession. How much money I was going to make was never discussed.

My parents didn't talk about money, but I think they worried about it. They never had a lot. I'm sure they would have loved to have had more, but they did a lot with the meager funds they had. I was over twelve years old before my family owned an automobile. I remember it was gray and squarely built. I believe it was called an Essex-Terraplane. In 1940, my daddy bought a Plymouth and it lasted until way after the Second World War. After the war he bought a Pontiac. I inherited the Plymouth. I went to Georgetown in 1949 in my 1940 Plymouth. It was a good old car.

I had a couple of job offers before I graduated from Newberry. There were ninety-seven of us in the Class of '49, the college's largest in its history at that time, thanks to the G. I. Bill. I had interviews in Manning, Summerville, and Georgetown. I don't know why I went with Georgetown, maybe because my parents had met in Kingstree and that was thirty miles away. But it was a great experience for me.

I was hired to teach high school math and physics and to be the head basketball and baseball coach, and assistant football coach. There was no Georgetown High School. It was Winyah High. The black high school was Howard. My baseball team played at the city ballpark, and that was within two blocks of Howard High School, but it was on the other side of the park, and I didn't worry about it. That was the mentality at the time. William Bynum, who was the school superintendent before I got there, had dictated that the "Battle Hymn of the Republic" would not be played. Though he was gone before I got there, that restriction was still enforced. I was hired by Henry White, the current superintendent at the time.

It didn't take long to learn that in Georgetown football was the only sport of value. When any of the boys went downtown, the merchants would say, "Son, what grade you in? You playing football?" If you didn't play football, then you didn't matter quite as much. Ed McLendon was the head coach and athletics director. When he left the next year, I was named athletics director. At twenty-three, I was still the baseball coach, basketball coach, and taught five classes too.

I didn't want to coach football. I was good at fundamentals, but I didn't want to get into the day-by-day aspects of coaching, so I hired Cecil Woolbright to be head football coach. That was probably one of the best decisions I made in Georgetown. He was a hell of a coach. Cecil was waiting tables at the Market Restaurant in Columbia; he'd been captain of USC's football team in 1950. He had a wife and needed some money. He continued Winyah's successful football program.

After a few years, family health problems caused Cecil to leave Georgetown for Arizona. When he came back to South Carolina, he coached at Cardinal Newman in Columbia and then in Chapin. Chapin's football field is the Cecil Woolbright Stadium. Ed McLendon ended up in Winnsboro, and Fairfield Central's stadium is named for him. At my next job, in Beaufort, I hired Lonnie Armstrong, who played for Clemson, to be our assistant football coach. The stadium at Mid-Carolina is named for him. All of these coaches are great people, and they all lived within forty miles of each other. Maybe there's something in the air—and maybe someday there will be a Dufford Stadium!

∽

Because such a high premium was placed on football, I didn't inherit a good basketball program. My first year in Georgetown, we won three basketball games of about twelve. This was the pre-Frank McGuire era in South Carolina. There weren't basketball goals in driveways. There was just one gym. Players didn't have experience and there weren't junior high teams on which to get any. For many of the students, the first time they touched a basketball was when they tried out for the high school team. Some of them weren't good enough to play other sports, and others just wanted something to do in the winter. Back then, each school sport was three months long and there weren't any summer camps. Basketball was something you did between football and baseball.

I knew we had to do something if we were ever going to get better in basketball, so I took it upon myself to develop a program. I started Saturday morning clinics at the high school gym for junior high boys and organized a junior varsity team. I also started a summer basketball program with the town's recreation department. We'd play on their outdoor court on "The Point," an area on Winyah Bay. During those summers, I'd get four varsity players to choose their teams and coach open-court basketball. That way they could be playing basketball, get their hands on basketballs.

My second year the Winyah Gators won five games, and the third year we won nine. The fourth year we won sixteen, and the fifth we won eighteen. After the third year, we won between sixteen and twenty of our twenty-two-game season. We were able to compete with schools in Charleston, which was the hotbed of basketball in the lower part of the state. Rural areas like Georgetown and Newberry were mainly football and baseball towns. We even had three basketball players chosen for All-Star Games at coaches' clinics—Larry Joe Bass, Bobby Rowe, and Arnie Brinson—just terrific kids.

I didn't mind spending my Saturdays and summers working with kids. Back then, you'd sign a contract for the year. You'd coach for nine or ten months and teach for 180 days. That was your contract. What I did in the summer and on Saturdays was on my own. I was doing what I wanted to do. I'd coach American Legion baseball, and most of those players were boys I coached and taught during the school year.

Sometimes I'd be asked to coach the girls basketball team when their coach got sick. Let me say this: I learned you coach girls basketball differently from boys basketball. You can be very critical of a boy on the court. You start doing that to girls, they take it personally. They'll say, "You don't like me." Oh my God. I was using the same technique I'd use with boys. It was the difference between night and day.

A few years later, after I'd been selected principal of Winyah Junior High, I came across two girls having a fight. They were in the girls' restroom in the school basement, and I heard them because I was walking the halls. I have no idea what they were fighting about, but they were pulling hair and pushing each other around. I tended not to make a big issue out of things like this, because human nature will lead people to act that way. I would sit the kids down and talk about expectations and say there are other ways to solve problems besides fighting. We didn't suspend them, but that would have been an easier way out for them than to have to listen to me. As you might have gathered by now, I can go on and on when I get started.

I remember most of my students by name, boys and girls. But the girls whose names I don't remember and probably never knew were the daughters of Josh Wright. From 1953 until 1958, he was the custodian at Winyah Junior High. Josh was a great fella, very dependable, and he had three girls who went to Howard High School, the mandated all-black high school. When they got out of school every afternoon, they would come over and clean up the white school. Can you imagine the reverse—three little white girls going over to clean up the black school? Those kids were good, and they helped their daddy. They would move all those heavy desks around to sweep the floors, and when they got through late in the afternoon, 5:30 or 6:00, Josh and his daughters would go home to the black community.

∽

Television was just starting to become popular when I moved to Georgetown, and the lady I rented a room from, Rose Grimm, had a black-and-white set in her living room. When I'd come home at night after coaching a game, she and her boyfriend would be watching boxing matches. Sometimes I'd watch with them, but mainly my life was busy with school, sports, and kids.

In 1952 I bought my first car, a new blue Studebaker with red wheels. It was from Camlin Motors in Georgetown; Mr. Camlin had sons who played football. A car was important because there were an awful lot of people from off in the country who played athletics, and they had to get home. I would take kids home after basketball and baseball practice, and some would hitchhike to Murrells Inlet, Pawleys Island, down almost to McClellanville. They couldn't drive; they didn't have cars. Girls would practice after school from 3:00 to 5:00, and we would practice from 5:30 to 7:30.

That Studebaker took me and some of those kids other places. During the summers, I'd take a few boys I'd coached and taught to Washington, D.C., and New York to see the sights and a baseball game. I needed a vacation and I needed company, and the parents wanted to get rid of the kids. In Washington we'd visit the Lincoln and Jefferson Memorials, and of course the Washington Mall. But my favorite story is from when we went to the Washington Zoo. We passed a fenced-in area with a sign that said "Dangerous for electricity." Sonny Brown, a rising senior, had fun with that first word. "Danger-oos," he said, rhyming it with "kangaroos."

We always went to a professional baseball game on those trips, and were fortunate enough to see Ted Williams and John Parnell, a great pitcher for the Red Sox. One year, as we were about to go into the Holland Tunnel to New York City, we saw a man in uniform signaling to the traffic. Here we are country boys, and I thought he was a lawman because of his uniform. He wanted to sell us tickets for a tour around New York Harbor, so we bought some. We were up there to watch the Detroit Tigers play the Yankees, and the day we took that tour the Detroit pitcher threw a no-hitter against the Yankees—and we were on a boat around the harbor. Virgil Trucks pitched the no-hitter. The tour was a great experience, but it was the wrong time to take it.

One of the boys on those trips was Reed Swann. I coached him in baseball and taught him in physics, and listened to him on the radio when he worked as a high school deejay on WGTN in Georgetown. I had no idea at the time that Reed and I would crisscross each other throughout our lives. He became a wonderful friend and colleague. But he's still one of my kids—even if he's past eighty now and has grandkids himself.

～

What I figured out back then, as a young teacher and coach in my first job, is that teachers become almost like parents to their students. I wasn't much older than they were, but I was old enough to see different groups among the kids and different groups in the town. Some had more than others, and some had very little. Many came from humble backgrounds, and their parents worked hard. International Paper was the big employer, and people worked long shifts there, coming home very late. Some downtown families were well off enough that the mothers didn't need to work outside the home. But the parents made sacrifices for their kids and we teachers were dedicated to our students.

As leaders of Winyah Junior High, we realized we were getting kids who weren't reading on grade level. We tried to find books that covered the same content but used language they could understand. In those days, there were no resources for help, no programs from the South Carolina Department of Education, no district curriculum consultants. We had teachers: Margaret Poole, Frances Bynum Clary, Eleanor Poston, and Arthur Doyle. We'd meet after school to try to figure how we could help these kids succeed. Reading problems were causing too many kids to be held back. One boy stayed in eighth grade two years because he couldn't pass math, and he couldn't pass math because he had a hard time reading the word problems. None of us got paid for staying late, and we knew the school district didn't have money for tutors. But we were all concerned about our students being able to succeed and make their way in the world.

I was starting to learn that I wanted all students, no matter their backgrounds or intelligence or how they fit in with others, to have a chance at life and get an education. To me, they were all part of the family and they all deserved fair treatment.

⁓

Winyah High was like most high schools of that era, which was different from how I went to school. These kids had to complete twelve grades before graduating, and public school lunch had been implemented. Winyah High, which included grades seven through twelve, had grown too big, so Winyah Junior High, then a new concept, was introduced for grades seven and eight. In 1953, Superintendent Henry White asked me to become its principal.

The junior high was next door to the high school in what had been the old elementary school until a new elementary school was built less than a mile away. Having a side-by-side high school and junior high made it easy to ramble between both schools during recess and between classes. Rambling's a great way to learn about what's going on in schools. That's how I came across those girls fighting in Georgetown, and boys smoking in the bathroom years later in Sumter. Many principals in those days stayed in their offices and read the paper. But I liked getting out and seeing what my basketball boys were doing with their free time. Because I was the principal, I didn't have to teach classes, but I was still coaching high school basketball and baseball, and I was still the athletic director of the high school. And for some reason, the teachers had elected me president of the Georgetown County Education Association. It was rare for a coach to get that position.

One day during recess, I looked out the window and saw our junior high kids making fun of Alex Alford, a local African American man who sold peanuts out of a basket. Everybody called him Peanut. He was disabled and probably had some mental deficiencies. I rang the bell and we had an assembly, and we talked about expectations for student behavior. I said I never wanted to see that type of behavior again. I don't know if the kids were picking on Alex because he was black or because he had a physical impairment, but I was really irritated about how our middle school kids treated this person on the sidewalk by the school. We shouldn't treat anybody that way, I told them.

Don't think I'm any kind of hero. There were all kinds of things going on in the world that I wasn't paying attention to. In the early 1950s, when I was learning how to be a teacher and coach, black parents in Clarendon County were putting their jobs and lives on their line so their kids could get a school bus. Some of those kids were walking eight miles to school and eight miles back. Blacks never wanted much, they just wanted to be treated fairly. Their court case was *Briggs v. Elliott*, and right around then is when the South Carolina General Assembly set up a Segregation Committee led by Senator L. Marion Gressette to keep the state's black and white schools separated.

Then, when the Supreme Court ruled in 1954 that "separate is inherently unequal" and that schools would have to integrate, you would never have known that anything happened. There were no epistles from the superintendents or school boards about how we were going to deal with this change and obey the law. The thinking was, if you don't talk about something, it didn't happen. They wanted to keep living like they had in the Jim Crow era.

But *Brown v. Board of Education* only made white southerners dig their heels in harder. Instead of trying to abide by the law, most states in the South and most school boards in the South fought against integration rather than trying to prepare for integration, which caused the problem to be greater than it was. In Georgetown, we went on with our daily practices at school. We rang the bell and went to homeroom. We went through our six periods and then went home. And everybody was happy. Well, everybody in the white community was happy.

∽

I was in hog heaven in Georgetown, and could have stayed there the rest of my career. But like many people in my profession, I felt the expectation to advance. So I started working on a master's degree and spent part of my summers in Columbia at the University of South Carolina, staying in the Preston dorm. One of my professors there would have a huge impact on my life, not that I could have known it then.

Dr. L. C. McArthur—he went by "Currie"—was an adjunct education professor at USC during that summer, and he was superintendent of schools in Beaufort. We must have discussed my job as principal of the new junior high in Georgetown or I wrote a paper about it, because he called in 1956 to see if I'd come be the principal at the new junior high school being established in Beaufort. Not having my master's degree yet, I wasn't qualified. But he called again the next year, and this time I had completed my master's.

I talked with the superintendent in Georgetown, and he said if I went to Beaufort I'd get higher pay, a secretary, and I wouldn't have to coach basketball or baseball. All I'd have to do is be a principal. In his wisdom, Ed Eaddy, the superintendent of schools at that time, said I'd have to make a decision to either stay with coaching or stay with administration. That was the decision that had to be made.

He was right. With all the conditions presented to me, I chose to go to Beaufort. I'd never been to Beaufort, never worked for Dr. McArthur, and I was leaving this great situation in Georgetown where people held me in high regard. I remember some of my basketball players coming to see me, to ask if there was some way they could get me to stay. But I'd gotten my master's in education in 1955, and my mother had been killed in a car accident in 1953. Maybe I felt like it was time for a new chapter, or more responsibility.

Either way, I was leaving a time of innocence. I would never teach homeroom again or have the experience of singing with those girls in ninth grade. I wouldn't have the freedom that came with working at a small school with a limited budget, allowing me to take my physics class outside to play touch football because there wasn't enough equipment for the lab period. But I had started a tradition of class trips—from driving my Studebaker with a few boys to Washington and New York to a school bus of boys to the Gator Bowl in Jacksonville in 1951. I was moving on. The times were too.

"When you think of Winyah High, you think of Bill Dufford"

Libby Doggett Bernardin took algebra from Bill Dufford. The 1952 Winyah High graduate, now a poet, remembers Dufford approaching her on the beach one summer. "He said, 'You have got to take my math class.' I was terrified of math as I was coming along in high school and still am. But he supported and encouraged you. He's amazing, he really is."

Harry Greenleaf, Winyah Class of '52, and his wife, Shirley Jordan Greenleaf, Class of '57, both were affected by Bill Dufford. "He taught me trig and I'm still doing it," Harry Greenleaf said.

Shirley Greenleaf has a strong memory: "Bill chewed me out for crossing the gym floor in Weejuns. He scared me so badly."

She remembers the crushes all the girls had on him. "The freshman girls loved him. When you think of Winyah High, you think of Bill Dufford."

"I just aggravated him," says Lula Mae Mitchum Anderson, Winyah Class of '52. Her favorite Bill Dufford story is when he sent her and two football players to the board to work a math problem. The problem was frustrating, and Anderson kept trying to figure it out. "I threw an eraser at Bill Dufford. I thought I would be expelled."

She wasn't, and like others, she became his friend. "He is one of the best to come out of Winyah High School. He was fair to everybody and he tried to work with each of us."

"He didn't put up with bad behavior and I think a lot of behavior was changed because of Bill," says Doug Corkern, a 1953 Winyah graduate. A retired architect on Hilton Head Island, Corkern played catcher on the baseball team Dufford coached. In a game with Myrtle Beach High, Corkern took action about a Myrtle Beach player who'd filed his metal cleats.

"He cleated me coming into home plate after cutting the pants leg on our second and third basemen. I jumped on the guy, and his brother came out of the stands and pulled me off of him. Coach Dufford threw me out of the game for fighting, and the umpire threw the Myrtle Beach player out."

In hindsight, Corkern recognizes Dufford's "lessons were mostly off the field in the game of baseball." One particular lesson involved his throwing orange peels under the school building after lunch. Corkern thought it was okay because they were biodegradable. Dufford disagreed. "He saw it as trash and made me go get it. I have never thrown anything resembling trash on the ground again."

"You wanted to play your butt off"

Gerald Freeman can still see his Winyah High School basketball coach at work on the court. Bill Dufford would lean forward, jabbing his right index finger into his left palm to make his points.

"You didn't want to mess up. He was so demanding and he put some-thing in you that made you want to please him. He's probably the one adult in my life that, outside of my father, I would dread him knowing something bad about me. You don't want Coach Dufford to know you were screwing up."

Hungry to play and not that talented, Freeman "had to work my fanny off" to make the team in 1954. A junior guard, he didn't get much playing time that year. Boys on the bench avoided sitting by Dufford because some-times they bore the brunt of his intensity. Freeman experienced that intensity during a game with Charleston High. The Winyah Gators were running a fast break when the excited coach did something Freeman would never forget.

"He eased off the bench a bit, yelled something, and slammed his fist down. I jumped a bit, and then he clamped his teeth on my shoulder." Though wearing his team warmup jacket, Freeman found a bruise later.

Other times, the coach could be surprisingly kind. Freeman remembers the panic he felt when he realized he'd forgotten his shoes at a tournament in a College of Charleston gym. He was a senior then, and a starter. "I dreaded to tell him; he was going to jump down my throat. But I had to because time was running out. Coach stood there like he was going to come down, and then he said, 'That's no problem. Hang on a second.' And the College of Charleston equipment manager brought me some brand-new, white, size-ten Converse shoes. And he said, 'By the way, you're captain tonight.' That's the kind of guy he was. You wanted to play your butt off."

"He'd be in the middle of it"

Phil Wilkinson played football for Bill Dufford at Winyah High. Growing up in rural Georgetown County, he helped his father a lot with manual labor. His father always made sure he drank plenty of water while working outside.

Coach Dufford believed differently. When Wilkinson drank water during practice, Dufford made him run laps. After running laps, Wilkinson drank more water. The scenario repeated itself until "he got furious and said, 'Don't you know why I'm giving you laps?' The thinking then was that you should be able to push through without water."

Wilkinson, a biologist and retired from the South Carolina Department of Natural Resources, played fullback for Winyah for three years. "I thought Dufford was a real good coach. He explained what we were going to do and why, so it would make the team click."

Because Dufford coached, taught, and helped students with other activities, Wilkinson and his classmates became personal friends with him. "We'd go by and visit him, and if there was a parade or festival, he'd be in the middle of it. But he was a very exacting teacher. You didn't get by with stuff just because you were friends with him. When it came time to snap the football, it was all business. When it was time to take the test, you better pass."

"It was a gesture he could make"

For Nell Morris Cribb, Bill Dufford will always be "Mr. Dufford." That's how she addressed him in 1958 as his secretary at Winyah Junior High, and that's how she addresses him now.

"It's really a habit. You get in that mode at school, not to call anyone by their first name even if you grew up next door to them."

Though Cribb and Dufford spent only one year working together, they remain close. Both are regularly invited to class reunions in Georgetown. Cribb worked for the school district for thirty-one and a half years before retiring and starting Miss Nell's Tours. She knows she can count on seeing Dufford at funerals or other occasions involving their students. "He's right there for that family. Those students had parents who allowed their children to play sports under his direction and he had a lot of influence on them at their age, and he realized that."

In 2014, Dufford called Cribb to arrange a meeting with John Arthur Jones, the long-time custodian at Winyah High. Jones had retired after forty-three years, and Dufford couldn't attend the party Cribb had given him. So the threesome met at McDonald's on Pawleys Island.

"We had a little reunion of our own," Cribb said. "Mr. Dufford said to Johnny, 'I was a young man back then and in later years I realized you custodians, you ran the show. We couldn't be there without you to unlock the doors and lock them.' Johnny laughed and said, 'That was part of our job.' We had a nice visit. Dufford had bought this lovely card for Johnny and it had some money in it. He said, 'I just want you to know it's come to my attention that I should have done something long ago.' It was a gesture he could make at this stage in both of their lives and they realized it."

Jones passed away later that year. Josh Wright, the custodian at Winyah Junior High, had died earlier.

"He wouldn't agree with what I'm going to say now, but he's very sentimental," Cribb said. "He was real concerned about the students and their welfare. He never boasted about buying a student basketball shoes if his family couldn't afford it. He wouldn't do something that would embarrass them or cause other students to realize what he was doing."

School was different in those Dufford days. "When I started out, the worst thing you could do is chew gum or smoke cigarettes," Cribb recalled. "Those were good years, I tell you."

Chapter 10

◠

Two Homecomings in Two Years

I DON'T KNOW how you view your life, but mine was not planned. And those two years between 1958 and 1960 were a real roller coaster, because I left Georgetown for Beaufort to establish a junior high school, then went to Newberry College as an assistant football coach and education professor, then came back to Beaufort as the high school principal. I'd call that pretty crazy, but I learn something everywhere I go.

When I got to Beaufort as the junior high school principal, I realized it was a whole different community from Georgetown. Beaufort had the military bases, which meant families came and went, and those families had children who were more cosmopolitan because they'd lived in other places. Georgetown was more rural and stable, with families that had been there for years. The parents worked for International Paper and were unionized. But in Beaufort I was still working with seventh and eighth graders, and that's my favorite age group. They're more open, more honest, more amenable. It's just a great age to deal with kids.

At that time it was alright to paddle kids if they'd done something wrong, and one day I needed to paddle Freddie Trask. He'd written a poem that was disparaging about his teacher, and she sent him to me to discipline. I said, "Freddie, you really shouldn't be doing this. I have to give you a little paddling." I had a plastic chair in my office, and like I did with every kid, I asked Freddy to step near it. I would paddle him a little, and then I would hit the chair. That way, if anybody asked "What did he do to you?" the kid could truthfully say "He paddled me." He just didn't have to say how hard.

After I'd disciplined Freddie and sent him back to class, his daddy came to visit Dr. McArthur the next day in the superintendent's office. The Trasks were a wealthy farm family from Wilmington. Dr. McArthur called me and said, "John Trask is in my office and would like to talk to you." I said, "Tell him I'm in my office; I look forward to talking to him. He can come to my office." Mr. Trask never came by, but I think if you have a problem, you deal with the person you have a problem with. I was starting to realize Dr. McArthur and I had some differences when it came to dealing with people, particularly in regard to the principles of administration. He was a very smart man, had a doctorate from Columbia University in New York. He could quote from any number of studies. But there are exceptions to studies.

After a year as principal at Beaufort Junior High, I got a call from Harvey Kirkland, who was head football coach at Newberry College. He needed an assistant, and the college needed a guidance counselor and someone to teach in the education department. So Chris Kaufman, the college president, hired me to do all three roles. I was driving a '54 Plymouth by then, so I packed what little I had in it and moved back into our big house on College Street. My father was still working at Johnson-McCracken and keeping up his garden, although it was smaller now that he was older and there weren't as many mouths to feed. Virginia had moved back home and was teaching nearby, and C. A. had returned from service and had started his medical practice. We were all home again except for our sister Doris, and our mother.

Though the town hadn't changed much, Newberry College had grown. There were about 650 students that year. But it didn't seem well publicized that, as their counselor, I was there to help them figure out what they might do after graduation. What I did figure out was that

I wasn't cut out for full-time football coaching. By 1959, football had become a twelve-month job, and I didn't care about Xs and Os. Harvey Kirkland was a great fella; he'd say, "Let me show you a new scheme," and it was every day. I can deal with football for three months. Football should be pleasurable and enjoyable and not so time-consuming. But it's become the most important thing in colleges today. We've let it get away from us.

The year I was back in Newberry, Dr. McArthur got a job as super-intendent in Sumter and left Beaufort. J. M. Randel, the high school principal in Beaufort, had taken Dr. McArthur's job as Beaufort's super-intendent. Mr. Randel called me to take his old job as Beaufort's high school principal. So back in the Plymouth I went, but this time to a brand-new high school. Because I'd only been gone a year, it was more like a homecoming. The junior high students had moved up to the high school, and so had some of the teachers. I rented a room from Mrs. Bessie Levin and began working as assistant coach of the midget football team for the city's recreation league. The director was Basil Green, from Andrews, and he was coaching the team and handling the purchasing and managing the ball fields. I told him I'd help. When I was in Beaufort previously, I'd coached the Catholic Youth Organization's basketball team. It seemed I couldn't give up coaching, though I wasn't paid to do it.

Speaking of coaching, I can't help but think about the Cannon Street YMCA Little League baseball team in Charleston. In 1955, the team—made up of fourteen African American youngsters—won the Little League State Championship. Because the kids were black, they were not allowed to represent South Carolina in the league's run for the national championship. I mean, these kids were not allowed to go because they were black! And that's why the Dixie Youth Baseball League was born, to form a different league so that the black kids wouldn't represent South Carolina. The Cannon Street story helped me realize what was happening in my home state. I think what happened to those black boys became part of my evolution from "the way it is" to "that's not the way to treat people."

❧

The new Beaufort High School had been built on Mossy Oaks Road, several miles from the old one. It had a well-equipped home economics department with fancy refrigerators and washers, dryers, and stoves. It also had a foreign language lab. Students could sit in booths and practice their French, and using a headset and recording device, the teacher could hear if they were enunciating correctly.

I was pretty fancy myself. I was making $6,000 more than I had in Georgetown, and I bought a big maroon early 1960s Chrysler from Von Harten Motors in Beaufort. It had big fins and was a big step up from the green two-tone Plymouth I'd been driving around.

Better than the Chrysler was the television in my office. I don't know why it was there, but it was invaluable, because I was able to see things that were going on in the broader world. We lived in peaceful Beaufort, but a lot of the South was in turmoil in the early 1960s. Because of that television, I could watch the coverage of the church bombing in Birmingham, the assassination of John F. Kennedy, the Freedom Riders, attempts at voter registration. I had a great view of the world because I had a television. It was the first one I ever had, and it was a color set.

When John Kennedy was shot and killed, it was 1:30 Eastern Standard Time. I probably would not have known he'd been assassinated if I hadn't had my television on. I watched the whole horrific event play out, replays of him getting shot and then being taken to Parkland Hospital.

This new president had built up an image in most people of great hope and great positive attitudes, and there wasn't this great divisiveness. We were looking at issues that were important. He talked about going to the moon. He was a real hero for people who had hope in the future that things would be brighter. It was a sad day.

Overall, though, Beaufort High was a paradise. It had a vibrancy because 25 to 35 percent of our student body was connected to the Marine Corps Air Station or Parris Island Recruit Depot, and they brought in new experiences. The parents were actively involved with the schools, and the school groups themselves were very active. My sixth and last year there, in 1965, Beaufort High was named a Pacesetter School for South Carolina by the National Education Association and *Parade* magazine; and in 1963 we had seven National Merit Finalists. Colonel Michael Ryan, whose three children were National Merit Finalists, said Beaufort High was the best school his children had attended from California to Virginia.

Our most notable military brat was a young man named Pat Conroy. Maybe you've heard of him. He came in the eleventh grade after being in private parochial schools all his life. His father, the colonel, had been transferred to the Beaufort air station. Because there were no Catholic schools within driving distance, the younger Conroy children attended the school at Laurel Bay, the Marine station's elementary school, and Pat enrolled at Beaufort High. When his daddy learned Pat had signed up for typing class, he came into the school office, wanting to know who enrolled his kid. My secretary, Norma Duncan, had enrolled him in his classes, but I didn't want her to have to deal with Pat's father. Protective of Norma, I said that I did. The colonel said, "My kid's not taking typing. He's not going to be a secretary." So we took him out of typing and put him in physics. Pat, a prolific writer, never used a type-writer. Throughout his life he wrote his manuscripts by hand.

Colonel Conroy wasn't mean-spirited in our conversation. He was just a demanding parent. But that wasn't my first introduction to Pat Conroy. My introduction came before school started, during a football scrimmage between Beaufort's junior varsity team and Laurel Bay's rec-reation league team. I was there observing, and the crowd was going crazy. There was a big kid from Laurel Bay who was running over Beaufort J. V. players as people cheered for him. "Skyhawk! Skyhawk!" Pat had never played football, so he didn't know the intricacies of the game. He was pretty husky, and he was taking it seriously. I thought, "This is a new kid coming into the community; he's making a big hit."

But he was a very humble, bright kid, and the kids and teachers loved him. After being there only one year, Pat was chosen to be presi-dent of the senior class, which is extremely rare. The president usually is someone who has been with a class all the years of their experience, but he had only been there one year. I don't think Pat wanted that honor, but his classmates saw him as kind of a leader and liked him so much. That decision reflected well on the student body, I thought, that they would be so open to accepting and rallying behind a new student. Pat was a great basketball player, but he also worked on the newspaper and literary magazine. He was voted Best All Around by his classmates.

Gene Norris, our junior English teacher, just adopted Pat. He saw more potential in him than most other people at the time. We saw him as gregarious, fun-loving, and easy to get along with, but Gene saw more underneath the surface and took Pat under his wing.

I did too, but not in any literary sense. The summer between his junior and senior years, he came to help me around the school. I let the guidance counselor and secretary take care of the next year's schedules, and Pat and I would cut grass, trim trees and shrubbery. He would hitchhike in every morning from Laurel Bay, and after he finished working with me, he was free to practice basketball in the gym. He'd played it in the Catholic schools. Pat wasn't a good shooter, but he could handle the ball real well. He was a great team player.

When Beaufort played Georgetown, I told my former players in Georgetown that we had a new kid on the team and "we are going to cut you." But Georgetown beat the hell out of Beaufort that night.

Pat's father would pick him up in the afternoon. I got to see the colonel every day. He was very pleasant. He'd ask, "How has your day been?" And he'd take Pat home. I didn't know about the things going on at the Conroy home then, but we all know them to be true now because of the great honesty of Pat's books.

Pat graduated and went to the Citadel in Charleston, but he kept in touch with me, Gene Norris, and other people in Beaufort. He later came back to teach at Beaufort High. There would come a time, after I found my true calling and tried to integrate schools in South Carolina, when I would ask something of Pat that would alter his life. But neither of us would have suspected that when we were cutting grass together around the high school.

Pat's not the only student from Beaufort who has made me proud. I think a lot of Alexia Helsley. She was Alexia Jones then, and editor of the high school paper her senior year. She's written twenty books and teaches history at USC Aiken. Her brother, Uel, was another fine student who rented from me in Columbia; he married Daisy Youngblood's sister. Daisy was one of my student office workers in Beaufort. She's a potter who won one of those MacArthur "Genius" Fellowships in 2003. And there's Sandi Mestler. After she graduated from Beaufort High in 1962, she went to the University of Alabama in Tuscaloosa. When Vivian Malone integrated that university in 1963—after JFK ordered George Wallace to step aside so she and James Hood could enter—Sandi agreed to be her roommate when no other woman on campus would. Her grandmother didn't want her to do that, said she worried she'd get a disease, and people stopped inviting her to parties. But Sandi held to her own convictions. Vivian Malone went on to be a great civil rights worker, and Sandi Mestler—McGarrah now—is a diaconal minister in the United Methodist Church in Charlotte. She teaches environmental stewardship to everybody from preschool children to retired adults.

I also must brag about Carl Epps, a lawyer in Columbia. He's another '62 graduate. He was the lead attorney for the forty poor school districts in South Carolina who sued the state in 1993 to provide an adequate education for their students. Carl stayed on that case for twenty-two years. I used to watch him in the Clarendon County courtroom in Manning, working to make our schools better. David Lauderdale quoted Carl in the *Island Packet* saying he learned more at Beaufort High School than he did in college. But maybe I shouldn't be surprised. After all, we had those seven National Merit Finalists in 1963. Over six years in Beaufort, two and a half percent of our students were National Merit Finalists; that was five times the national average!

Of course I know not all students have the same talents, academically or athletically. We realized many of the freshmen entering Beaufort High weren't reading on grade level. This was a problem I had faced in Georgetown in the 1950s, but we didn't have the resources to address it as well as I would have liked then. But Beaufort was different and we found a solution. Luckily, we had Louise Carson, who was director of elementary curriculum, and Gwen Johnson, who was certified to teach reading in the elementary and secondary levels. We brainstormed a plan to help those ninth graders and created our Developmental Reading Program. Miss Johnson taught those students English and social studies, and they used the same books as the other students. It was important that those ninth graders weren't singled out or embarrassed. But Miss Johnson needed more room for other books and materials, so we moved Gene Norris out of his classroom so she could have his. Gene was none too happy about the relocation, but that classroom had one of those old-fashioned cloakrooms and Miss Johnson needed that space for her extra books.

Our program worked, and soon most of those students were learning to read on grade level.

"You could tell he loved the kids"

As a young teacher at Beaufort High, Dutchin Hardin sought advice from Principal Bill Dufford, her algebra teacher in Georgetown. Teaching biology to accelerated ninth and tenth graders and then less capable eighth graders was a task she hadn't mastered.

"Bill helped me a lot in terms of knowing what I was dealing with and how to handle the situation," she recalls. "I didn't know how to teach and grade them, and he really helped me. He may not remember that, but I do."

Hardin wasn't the only teacher in Beaufort Dufford would help. In the late 1950s, she and eight other young, single teachers lived together in the "teacherage." They would talk later about how thankful they were to have started their careers under Bill Dufford. "He had utmost respect for the teachers and their decisions."

The respect went both ways, and with students too.

"He was fair. He didn't take guff from them," Hardin says. "He not only corrected them when they were doing something wrong, but he gave them compliments. You could tell he loved the kids and they knew that, and that sums up Bill Dufford. He was a dedicated teacher, dedicated to education, and dedicated to kids."

"I saw kids just blossom under him"

Norma Duncan was a young bride when she worked for Bill Dufford at Beaufort High School. A 1957 BHS graduate, she treasured working in the school she had also loved attending. As Dufford's secretary in the early 1960s, she observed how times were changing and how people reacted.

"We were on the cusp of integration and he was ready to embrace that, where other people weren't. He was looking beyond the box because he was so involved in wanting to have good education for everyone, not just the whites. He didn't know color. He was the most open-minded, open-hearted person I've ever been around."

Dufford's ability to single out students who weren't succeeding in the high school arena and make them feel good is one of his best attributes, Duncan said. "He loved sports and encouraged kids to participate in sports because that was a wholesome thing to do. I saw kids just blossom under him, just because he really, really cared."

Beaufort's new high school prompted pride in the building—pride that matched the respect students had for teachers and the love faculty and staff had for each other.

"It was just a special time," Duncan said. "We all cared so about each other, and the atmosphere in the office was that of happiness. Bill put his arms around the kids. They knew if they screwed up, they would be punished. But they so much respected Bill. There was so much respect, where today there's not much."

Chapter 11

❧

It Was Ugly in Your Head

A s I HAD SINCE CHILDHOOD, I went to church regularly, always joining whatever Lutheran church was in the town where I was living. I was a member of the church council at St. John's in Beaufort when the pastor, Dermon Sox, called a meeting of our council. An aviator from Minnesota was being transferred to the Beaufort air base, and he'd written Dermon a letter to introduce himself and ask if it would be okay for him, his wife, and two children to worship with us. In his letter, the aviator mentioned he was a lifelong Lutheran, and one other thing: he was black.

You would have thought an atomic bomb had been detonated in that room. The majority of the group was so vocal and so hostile to the idea of this black family worshiping with us that it would have been useless for Dermon and me to argue. In his wisdom, Dermon was just making the church council aware of this potential new member so no one would be surprised when a black family entered the sanctuary. This was 1964, and it was the rational and gentlemanly thing for a black person coming to the South to do, to write a letter saying, "I'm looking forward to being with you, and by the way, I'm black."

I think Dermon was just planning an informational meeting, but we ended up taking a vote. And that church council voted to tell that young man that every Sunday morning he needed to go to the closest black Lutheran church. That council did no research, but we found out later the closest black Lutheran church was in Alabama.

I was sitting there thinking, "Wait a minute, this is not what I learned in church. This is not what we teach kids." In church we're taught "God loves all people" and "the church is God's house." I haven't talked to anybody who wasn't taught that in their early church teachings, regardless of their denomination. And here we are telling a lifelong Lutheran that he needs to gather up his two kids and wife every Sunday morning and drive to Alabama to go to church. I realized what we were teaching and what we were doing were not the same, and the way we were living was crazy. I began to really understand that the mainstays of Jim Crow-era culture were not in keeping with the true teachings of

49

the church as I understood them, that we were keeping separate those who should be brought together.

Beaufort wasn't the only place where this kind of thing happened. I can tell you stories about Sumter and York and everywhere else where whites—particularly white men—were making sure blacks didn't go to *their* church. Not to God's church, to *their* church. Watch the descriptive words.

It was not an ugly meeting. Nobody struck anybody. But it was ugly in your head. The negativity really caught me off guard and it began to raise questions. I'd been watching television, seeing dogs unleashed on black people in Alabama and learning about Medgar Evers getting killed.

I don't think the congregation ever found out about what happened at that council meeting. Those people who voted against admitting that young man to the church probably told their wives, and their wives would have been proud of them. As far as I know, that aviator never visited St. John's, or wrote back.

Years later I met that preacher's son, Dermon Sox Jr. Like his father, he was a Lutheran minister. We talked about what happened at St. John's in Beaufort, and I found out Dermon Sr. had been through something even worse before he got to Beaufort. At St. Luke's Lutheran in Summerville, a black military family being transferred to Charleston inquired about worshiping with his church. When he brought it up, members of his church, some in law enforcement, threatened Dermon. So he was being slow and steady and very wise when he brought the black aviator's letter to the church council in Beaufort.

I kept going to St. John's, even after I recognized how differently I was beginning to think from other members on that church council. I felt like my preacher needed all the support he could get. I knew how he felt about it, and it was becoming clearer to me how I felt about it. What happened was wrong—just wrong.

"God's Church Should Be Open to Everyone"

Perhaps it should have come as no surprise that Pastor Dermon Sox Sr. was in favor of allowing African Americans to worship in white Lutheran churches. Almost sixty years earlier, his own father, Pastor David Adam Sox, had publicly and vehemently defended the rights of women to speak in the Lutheran church. David Adam Sox's beliefs surfaced in 1906—the year Dermon Sr.

was born—at the convention of the Synod of Georgia and Adjacent States near Plains.

Reportedly going against St. Paul, Martin Luther, and most congregations of the day, the fifty-year-old David Adam Sox thought so highly of Katherine Scherer Cronk's speech about her missionary work that he stood and moved to have her address published. The *Lutheran Church Visitor* then published a series of spirited letters about the subject by Sox and the disapproving Pastor Shepard Seneca Rahn.

Dermon Sox Sr. would have been sixteen when his father died in 1922, and nearing sixty when the African American aviator wrote him about visiting St. John's Lutheran Church in Beaufort. His son, Pastor Dermon Sox Jr., was shepherding his first church on Johns Island at the time. "He was a person who thought God's church should be open to everyone and that there should be no distinction," Dermon Sox Jr. said of his father. "As the Bible says, 'There is neither Jew nor Greek, there is neither slave nor free man, there is neither male nor female; for you are all one in Christ Jesus.'"

Dermon Sox Jr. would carry on his father's beliefs. At Gethsemane Lutheran Church in Columbia, he and his congregation welcomed their first African American couple in 1977. Gethsemane, with less than a hundred confirmed members, was one of the first Lutheran churches in the twentieth century to have African American members, the first to have an African American delegate to a Synod assembly, and possibly the first to elect an African American vice chair of the congregation—the highest lay office in the congregation. In 1993, Gethsemane—with Sox in the pulpit—became the first Lutheran church in South Carolina to officially welcome gay and lesbian members through the Reconciling in Christ program.

The success Sox and Gethsemane had with integration in the late 1970s prompted leaders at the South Carolina Lutheran Synod to ask him to serve on its Minority Ministry Task Force, frequently as chair, from 1980 to 1986. One of the first things the group did was send surveys to all Lutheran churches in the state to gauge their attitudes toward African Americans and the possibility of welcoming them to worship. Few responded. Those who did took offense to the surveys.

"Mostly it was pastors filling them out, and some were very racist in their outlook. One pastor in particular told me, 'By your actively working toward racial inclusivity, you have excluded yourself from being invited to be a pastor in most churches in South Carolina.'"

Sox shrugs off any notion that it took courage to preach openness to all people and chair the task force. "I didn't see it that way. I saw it as something I had to do. I guess I'm my father's son."

Chapter 12

❧

The Path Gets Clearer

B Y 1964, when the dangers of Jim Crow were becoming clearer to me, ten years had passed since the Supreme Court mandated all southern schools integrate "with all deliberate speed." School boards, normally priding themselves on being Christian, law-abiding people, began finding ways not to integrate, mainly by opening private, Christian "academies." Intermingling between blacks and whites was unacceptable to those people, because then blacks would be equal. Whites needed to keep thinking they were superior.

What happened "with all deliberate speed" in public schools was "Freedom of Choice." From 1964 to 1970, a few black students could go to white schools if they were permitted to, and a few black teachers could teach in white schools. You had to be a brave person to be black and come to a white school. You wouldn't see a white person going to a black school. I'm sure they had good teachers, but their books, gyms, libraries, labs—all their facilities—were much worse than what the white schools had. And remember that the African American schools at the time were under the direction of all-white school boards and superintendents.

Rowland Washington was Beaufort High School's first black student. He enrolled in 1964, by himself, without his parents. He was accepted by most of the kids, but I'm sure when teachers weren't around there was some picking and shoving. One day Mike Lapatka, the center on the football team, came to me at lunch; he said, "Come out here. Rowland Washington shouldn't have to put up with this." I hurried to the area between the cafeteria and gymnasium, but I didn't see anything physical, just kids jabbering. They dispersed when they saw me coming. I asked Rowland if he was okay, but he never complained.

From my standpoint, race relations in Beaufort were pretty peaceful. That wasn't true elsewhere in South Carolina. In 1961, seventy-five Benedict College students participated in a sit-in at Woolworth's in Columbia. Hayes Mizell, a white man and program associate of the American Friends Service Committee, joined them. Hayes became a friend and ally of mine years later, when I moved to Columbia. Also that year, "The Friendship Nine," nine black students at Friendship

Junior College in Rock Hill, were arrested for sitting at McCrory's all-white lunch counter. Harvey Gantt of Charleston became the first black student at Clemson University in 1963. Also in 1963, the General Assembly in South Carolina passed the Tuition Grants Act, which gave $225 in tuition grants to public school students who wanted to go to private schools. That act was found illegal by the U.S. Fourth Circuit Court of Appeals after the National Association for the Advancement of Colored People and the U.S. Department of Justice filed suit. In hindsight, I'm not too proud of this state.

I know Pat Conroy wrote about my earlier feelings about the races being separated. When the Supreme Court ruled in 1954 that schools should integrate, I believed like most southerners did—that they shouldn't. As a young educator, that's what I thought. That's how we were raised in the South. But I was really changing. And the best professors I would ever have in my life would help me get over the line to where I knew how I thought, and I was ready to take the action to match.

~

One of those professors was Herb Way. He was dean of the College of Education at the University of Miami. I met him during the summer of 1964, when I was renewing my certification at Western Carolina University in North Carolina. I think the course was Audio Visual Aids—how you turn on a 16-millimeter projector, pull a screen down. He said, "You ought to come down to the University of Miami, I'll give you an assistantship." I had never thought of going to the University of Miami. I didn't even know what an assistantship was. But I just tucked that way in the background. He'd planted a seed, not that I knew it then.

After summer school, I went back to Beaufort to start my sixth year as the high school principal. At that time, there were pre-school conferences for teachers. They were really pep talks for the coming year, and there was always an important guest speaker. That year our speaker was Kimball Wiles, dean of the College of Education at the University of Florida. He was a dynamic, great speaker. As the principal, I sat with him. Dr. Wiles said, "You need to come to the University of Florida, I'll give you an assistantship." I never applied, never thought about it. But in two months I got two offers for assistantships in Florida. "Okay," I said, "I'll think about it."

I was not the most ambitious academic pursuer. I never found schooling to be difficult, and I could get by on doing what I had to do.

But as the year went on, I got to considering that earning my doctorate might be a good thing, but which university should I choose? That was the big dilemma. This was the kind of thing you should put a lot of thought into; you get out the books and plan. I did none of that. I knew I'd get a good education no matter where I went. I chose to go to the University of Florida, because it was in Gainesville and closer to South Carolina. I didn't want to get too far from home. I had had that navy experience and I was not too adventuresome.

It was hard to leave Beaufort, where, like Georgetown, I was in hog heaven. Mrs. Levin made me coffee and breakfast every morning and cookies and snacks on Saturdays. It was so easy living there; I didn't even have my own telephone line. Can you imagine a high school principal not having a phone?

It's interesting to think back now that the teachers in Beaufort, like the teachers in Georgetown, elected me president of their association. It was rare for a principal to lead a teachers' group, just like it was unusual for a coach to do so. But they wanted me to handle those duties, so I did. This has been a theme in my life. I've just kind of fallen into roles and responsibilities that I didn't actively seek. But being the president of the teachers' associations in Georgetown and Beaufort meant a great deal to me as a sign of trust and respect on the part of those who elected me.

Leaving Beaufort also meant no more senior class trips to Washington and New York. One year a couple of students, Brett Bursey and a buddy of his, caused a loud ruckus in the science wing. Brett wouldn't tell me who his friend was for me to discipline them both, so I said he couldn't go on the class trip. "If I can't trust you in Beaufort, I can't trust you in New York," is what I told him. And I returned his fee for the trip.

To his credit, Brett didn't rat on his friend. I'm not sure he wasn't more noble than I was. But he didn't like not getting to go. We got a call the day before we were going to make the trip. The person on the other line said, "This is Captain Bursey. If my son doesn't make that trip, nobody will make it. I'll blow the train up in Yemassee." And he hung up. Brett's daddy was a dentist and a captain in the navy. Well, ain't no captain going to make a call like that, but I didn't know at the time if we'd get blown up. I think Brett got somebody to make that call. If it had been Brett we would have recognized his voice.

Those trips were a highlight of the year, but the kids had to pay to go. The poorer kids couldn't afford it, so there was a sense of unfairness.

❧

Beaufort in the Early 1960s: "An Extraordinary Educational Experience"

To Alexia Jones Helsley, the Beaufort Class of '63 senior trip was one for the record books. Washington, D.C., and New York City were entertaining enough on their own, but drop some real hometown characters into those cities and the laughs would last for a lifetime.

First there was English teacher Gene Norris. He encouraged Helsley, the quiet, studious daughter of a Baptist minister, to hit the sleeping Pat Conroy with a pillow while traveling to Washington by train. The friendship that developed between the two classmates grew when Conroy and a friend composed a poem, "Ode to Sexy Lexy," on toilet paper perfumed with English Leather. Later, in Washington, Helsley joined a few other adventurous students on an unscheduled visit to the National Gallery of Art. Norris, ever intent on broadening his students' lives, led the tour. After leaving the museum, they had to run to catch the bus that was taking off without them.

In New York, the students visited the United Nations and Radio City Music Hall, where they saw the Rockettes and the movie *Gypsy*. "'Let Me Entertain You' became our theme song," Helsley recalled. But nothing was more entertaining than watching Bill Dufford discipline Conroy and another student in the "dubious" neighborhood in which they were staying. Eating supper at a Tad's Steakhouse, the 1959 *The Immoral Mr. Teas* playing in a theater nearby, Dufford began counting heads. He realized students were missing.

"And he looks out the window and sees Conroy and another friend sauntering across one of those big broad avenues and he charges across the street and stops traffic. He blesses them out in the middle of the street and horns are blaring. They had violated protocol. Nobody knew where they were. It was a hoot to see."

That sort of authoritative action wouldn't have surprised anyone; students knew Dufford was a disciplinarian who didn't hold back on his opinion or affection. Like her classmates, Helsley was amazed that a principal would step out into the hallways, talk to students, know each one by name. "We never had that in elementary school. I only knew who the principal was because he lived across the street from us and was a member of our church. He didn't come visit your classroom and speak to you. Bill Dufford did."

Dufford recruited and hired first-rate teachers, and stood behind them, Helsley said. When some parents in her father's congregation complained about Norris assigning *The Catcher in the Rye*, Helsley defended him. So did her father, Dr. George A. Jones, and so did Bill Dufford. Norris's class read the book.

Nor was there any administrative interference with *The Tidal Wave*, the high school newspaper Helsley edited. When her good friend Julie Zachowski drew a cartoon of a hooded Klansman with the scythe of death on his shoulder, Helsley ran it with no problem.

"I think because of Dufford, we had an extraordinary educational experi-ence," she said. "The principal sets the tone, and if the principal is paying atten-tion, things go well—*if* he or she is competent. And he was very competent."

Now living near Columbia and a historian, archivist, and author of twenty books, Helsley can't help but think her stories about Beaufort High filtered to her son and daughter. Their school experiences in Irmo were vastly different, simply because of size. But she watches her daughter, the principal at Oak Point Elementary in Lexington-Richland District 5, and wonders if Cassandra Helsley Paschal didn't somehow channel Bill Dufford's energy and manage-ment style. "Those ideas are carried forward. Cassie knows the names of all the students she ever had. She will call these kids, after they're in middle and high school, by name, and they're all running up and hugging 'Mrs. Paschal.' It's phenomenal to me."

Gainesville was a great, great setting for a university and the University of Florida was a beautiful university. I was a forty-year-old graduate assistant working on my doctorate in curriculum and instruction, and about to experience the best teaching I ever had. Let me tell you my def-inition of great teaching: one who gets the student interested in what's being discussed in the classroom—really involved in it.

I wasn't back in school to learn about the unfairness of Jim Crow, but two professors in particular made me understand it in terms I could no longer ignore. Hal Lewis and Vince Hines talked about black people who'd left the South because they couldn't find work and went north to find jobs during the Depression. Then, when they wanted to come back and visit their families, they could find no place for lodging, no place for meals, no place to go to the bathroom. Family in the black commu-nity is very important, probably more so than in the white community. But it was just a struggle for them to visit. Those professors would tell stories about the cruelty of segregation and separation, and they would almost be crying, talking about what people had to do just to come back and visit their families.

What they talked about were things I had been living through and been blinded by in a Jim Crow society. They really brought it into focus. And these were two old southern boys, fellas who'd grown up in the South. They weren't Yankees, but they were able to convey that message. After what I'd been watching and thinking about in Beaufort, then coming to the University of Florida in 1966–1967, it was like a bucket of water being thrown on me. It really woke me up. This world I had been living in was unjust, and the awareness of that was a moment of profound sadness for me. But it also kindled a fire in me to change things if I could.

Another great teacher I had was Art Combs. His field was educational psychology, and he wrote a great little book, *Perceiving, Behaving, Becoming.* When you perceive something, you behave a certain way, and then you become that way. His course and that book were another part of my evolution. They weren't explicitly about human cruelty, but they put the pieces together in my mind about why people act the way they do.

Now we have books like *Out-of-the-Box in Dixie* by Cecil Williams, a photographer in Orangeburg who covered the civil rights movement, and *Free at Last* by Sara Bullard, about those who worked and died for civil rights. We didn't have books like that, even when I was in Florida.

∼

During that time in Florida I had five professors—William Alexander, Art Combs, Glenn Haas, Vince Hines, and Kimble Wiles—who either were or had been presidents of the ASCD, the Association of Supervision and Curriculum Development, which was the big organization in the field of education. This was a really high-powered group. My major professor was Dr. Alexander, and he was famous across the country for designing curricula and developing middle schools. Middle school was a brand-new concept for kids going into adolescent years, which is a very crucial age. Junior high schools never dealt with that.

I was one of about a dozen graduate assistants for Dr. Alexander and Dr. Hines, a statistics professor. They were working with the Southern Association of Schools and Colleges, which had given the University of Florida a grant to research what changes had been made at the schools that had undergone SASC accreditation. Our team's job was to interview and survey school administrators and teachers in fifty schools from Miami to Atlanta to see whether curriculum changes had created school improvement. Those interviews were a good opportunity to get out and see schools and come back and compare notes.

One school I visited was the Miami Military Academy, a secondary school for boys. I had my checklist of things to ask. When I asked the commandant if his teachers were certified, he said, "Most of our teachers aren't certified, but they're all qualified." I'll never forget that.

The school was having a dress parade when I was there, and the commandant wanted me to judge which platoon performed and looked best. I was in no military raiment, but I was the honored guest to choose the best platoon. I was saying to myself, "What the hell is going on here?" I understood what the man was doing. It wasn't a good school, academically, but they wanted to put their best foot forward, thinking that would shape my idea of who they really were.

I based my dissertation on what we learned from that research. I wanted to see if the way the principal behaves makes a difference in curriculum change across an organization. My study found there was no significant difference governed solely by the behaviors of the principal in how schools responded as organizations when curriculum changed. The principal could be dogmatic, democratic, or laissez-faire.

One night when I was driving back to Gainesville from Miami, I picked up WBT in Charlotte on the radio. WBT was a so-called "clear channel station," which meant its signal could be directed into Cuba. Reed Swann, my former student from Georgetown, was on the air. He didn't announce his name until later in the hour, but I knew his voice because we'd kept in touch over the years. Reed had always done a little moonlighting in the broadcasting business, and by this time he was teaching and coaching in York County and trying to make a little extra money. I wondered how Charlotte, North Carolina, was being picked up in Orlando, Florida. Everybody has kind of a unique voice. I probably hadn't seen Reed in ten years, but I knew it was him.

Maybe it was hearing that familiar voice, or maybe it was not being interested in going to Chile when Bill Alexander said I could be that country's Administrator of American Schools. Either way, I was ready to go back home. I'd earned my doctorate in curriculum and instruction, and my classmate Steve Spurrier had won the Heisman. UF football games were great, but not enough for me to stay. I hadn't joined a church, either, so I had far fewer roots in Florida than I had in South Carolina.

"All of us had to change"

Even when Bill Dufford didn't look like he was working, he was. In Beaufort he started at breakfast.

"That's when he politicked," said Millen Ellis, a longtime English teacher at Beaufort High. The town's influential men gathered at Harry's Restaurant downtown, where Dufford learned who was who and who could help. "One time I said I wanted to put flowers outside the window. All of a sudden this man brought in a truckload of azaleas."

Once Dufford was criticized for not being at school before the teachers arrived. "That didn't bother him," Ellis said. "Everybody knew what was going on. He did it on purpose." Dufford, he said, was a master at hiring responsible people and delegating accordingly. Department chairs and class heads kept things running efficiently, and faculty members voted on policy. Unlike some principals Ellis worked for in his nearly forty years of teaching, Dufford knew to learn from his teachers. As bachelors, Ellis and fellow teachers Walt Gnann and Joel West often had supper with Dufford. Their conversations around the table led to various practices Dufford used in school. "Bill would discuss things that would happen and he would get our input."

When Rowland Washington enrolled at Beaufort High in 1964, Dufford and his staff were ready. Not wanting the school's first African American student to feel uncomfortable, he devised a plan involving history teacher Grace Dennis. "He assigned her to be casually at the front door when he walked in, and then she casually, as if bumping into him, said she would guide him to the office. Bill avoided problems by anticipating them."

Dufford left Beaufort about five years before full integration occurred in 1970. Ellis recalled a time of "mass activity" when the black students from the large, downtown Robert Smalls High and the small, isolated Saint Helena High merged at the mainly white Beaufort High. There had been none of the preparation—black and white teachers meeting to discuss curriculum and policy—that Dufford initiated in Sumter, where he was at the time.

"They threw us together," Ellis said. "The establishment, the power structure of Beaufort, were hoping integration would be a failure so they could say we told you so. Had Bill been there it would have been a whole lot smoother than it was. It wouldn't have been perfect, but he would have been able to talk with black students. He would have made them feel as if they were important and part of the school and eliminate the resentment of leaving their school."

Ellis and his teacher friends knew the University of Florida made a big difference on their principal and friend. It was obvious when he visited them in Beaufort. "He was a changed man. I don't know that anybody talked about racism, but Bill Dufford met it face to face. All of us had to change—we had to—because it would have been difficult to teach a class of black students."

Chapter 13

∾

Lift Every Voice and Sing

My first opportunity to come home came from Charlie Williams, my Newberry College classmate. Charlie was the assistant state superintendent of education, and he had a three-year grant from the U.S. Department of Education to establish regional Educational Development Staffs to help schools integrate, develop their curriculums, and improve educational opportunities for kids. I specifically remember some of the language for our mission: to develop "innovative, creative, and exemplary programs." South Carolina was divided into seven regions, and I was assigned to Orangeburg. To get the funding from the grant, each of these regional offices was attached to a school district. I was tied in with Orangeburg District 5, where Bill Clark was superintendent.

The grant funded a good concept, but it wasn't realistic. I was the director of our staff, and I brought two of my doctoral classmates, Bob Braswell and Roger Webb, from the University of Florida to work with me. The three of us, with two secretaries, weren't enough to cover eight counties and the twenty-four districts within them. Our region included Aiken, Allendale, Bamberg, Barnwell, Calhoun, Lexington, and Orangeburg Counties, and Richland Districts One and Two. Some of those schools are very rural, and some are urban. To have three people help all those schools with programmatic development is basically impossible.

Of course we didn't realize that at the time. We immediately tried to figure out ways to help those schools. Bob and Roger and I decided to identify the best secondary, elementary, and early education schools in the country, and the most outstanding schools in arts and sciences. Then we contacted those schools and asked if we could visit them to learn about their programs. We flew twenty-four superintendents to Evanston Township High School in Illinois, the premier high school at the time. And we went to a terrific elementary school outside Pittsburgh, Pennsylvania, and the North Carolina School of the Arts in Winston-Salem. The preschool program we identified was in Sumter District 17.

We were hoping those other schools would trigger some thoughts about improving schools in our area.

This was during the 1967–1968 school year, and the Department of Health, Education, and Welfare began bearing down on these stubborn white school boards in the South. They'd been told in 1954 to integrate "with all deliberate speed," and many districts had done nothing more than continue to allow black students the "Freedom of Choice" to enter white schools if they wanted. Many school board members sent their own children to private, segregated schools.

Private schools were springing up in Orangeburg County too, but in District 5, where South Carolina State University is located, the racial atmosphere in the public schools seemed calm. I credit Superintendent Clark, who in his infinite wisdom had a terrific African American lady on his school board and an active African American assistant superintendent. This was a volatile time in South Carolina, and Orangeburg District 5 was the only place in the state I know of with African Americans in positions of authority. Dr. Clemmie Webber was that school board member; she was a professor at South Carolina State and a community activist. Dr. Robert Howard was the assistant superintendent. He became the first African American president of the South Carolina Principals Association.

Younger people, unfamiliar with how school and government politics worked before successful integration, might not understand why those two people were so important. But Clemmie Webber was a pioneer because blacks weren't allowed the right to vote until 1965. African Americans wouldn't have gotten into any system of politics when she was on the board in the late 1960s. Obviously she was well-enough respected in Orangeburg to win an election. As for Robert Howard, the key word in his title was *active* assistant superintendent. When schools were supposedly integrating—or rather, desegregating—many black administrators were transferred to white schools and given titles of authority. But "title" was where it ended. Those educators weren't allowed to make decisions. Robert Howard made decisions, and that was evident from the school board meetings in which he participated. There were other members on that board—Dr. Harry Atwell, a physician, and R. S. Williams, a druggist downtown—and they knew integration was coming. They had prepared as best they could.

Having such a progressive school board made a difference in February 1968, when the Orangeburg Massacre occurred on the campus of South Carolina State. Three students were killed, including one high school student. There were no real outbursts of hostility in the public school, and I give credit to Bill Clark and his staff and his board. I don't know what they did, but that would have been an opportune time for a school district to fall apart, and it didn't.

◦◦◦

There had been unrest in Orangeburg for three or four months leading to the killings at South Carolina State. All Star Bowling Lanes wouldn't admit blacks, and students had been protesting for days downtown. It was known something was going to happen. State Highway Patrol officers were there. I'm not sure how I heard about the shootings, probably on the radio. I had bought a house in a subdivision a couple of miles outside town and wasn't close to the activity.

There was a curfew, so people couldn't be out at night. You could go to work during the day, but there were troop carriers and weapons and the National Guard in the streets. Our staff wasn't involved with the investigation, but *Charlotte Observer* reporter Jack Bass and Jack Nelson, with the Washington bureau of the *Los Angeles Times*, used the conference room in our building to interview people who were. That room was on the back side of our office, so those being interviewed couldn't be identified entering and leaving.

The Orangeburg Massacre helped reinforce what I had learned and the evolution of my thinking with the great help of those professors at the University of Florida. Here I was, right back to white officials shooting black kids in the back, in South Carolina. Those African American students were being denied the right to go into a bowling alley. By that time, the Civil Rights Act had been passed. The owner of the bowling alley was breaking the law. *He* was violating the Civil Rights Act of 1964. But again, here was the state taking the side of the owner of the bowling alley. All of those law enforcement officers—the highway patrol, National Guard, SLED—were telling those black kids to go back on campus rather than telling that man to open up the business and let those kids in.

In the middle of all that uproar, something unforgettable happened. Chester Ray, the principal of Wilkinson High School, Orangeburg's black high school, invited me to his home. Black folks were gathering in different homes after the massacre, and he knew I was interested in successful integration. I think I was the only white person there. Before everybody left, we all joined together and sang "Lift Every Voice and

Sing." It's the black national anthem. I knew the tune, but they knew the words. They would sing it when they wanted to pledge allegiance to America, because they saw other songs as being a little hypocritical.

It's a great song and it was a sad time. I was moved because they all joined in. That was the first time I'd been invited to an African American's house. If anybody has ever been invited to a black group and made to feel anything other than comfortable, they need to come see me.

ᘓ

There was a lot for me to learn in Orangeburg, and there were people there, white and black, who impress me to this day. Superintendent Bill Clark isn't with us anymore, but he may be at the top. He was the old football coach at Orangeburg High School, and I got to know him when I was coaching in Georgetown. He grew up in Union. At athletic conferences, he would read books on philosophy, not football. Other coaches would be smoking cigars and talking about Xs and Os, but he'd be reading a book—which tells you he was above us. But he never imposed himself on the rest of us. He had a great personality, a very warm personality.

He was intelligent enough to see the handwriting on the wall, that integration was coming whether we wanted it or not. Bill Clark began to do things in South Carolina way before anyone else. And he caught heck for bringing Robert Howard from Wilkinson High to be the assistant superintendent.

But Robert Howard was just as impressive. He was born in Georgetown and came to Orangeburg as a student at South Carolina State. He got two degrees there before earning a graduate degree from George Peabody College, which is Vanderbilt now.

When Orangeburg and Wilkinson High Schools integrated, the names of both schools were kept. So were both principals. Neither lost his job, which is pretty decent. The new Orangeburg-Wilkinson High School was built to accommodate both student bodies. When the white principal learned he had to share administrative duties equally with the black principal, he left. But that's kind of typical.

I wasn't the only one to think highly Dr. Clark or Dr. Howard. Both have schools named for them in Orangeburg. When Robert "Wagg" Howard died in 2009, the funeral was at R. E. Howard Middle School.

Chapter 14

❦

Definitions

A LOT OF PEOPLE confuse "integration" with "desegregation," but they are not the same. Integration is when you bring two or more groups of people together in a setting that's comfortable and fair to everyone. In integration, everyone has a voice.

Desegregation is when you bring two or more groups of people together and put them in the same place. There's no fairness or concern for others. It's about geography.

By the spring of 1969, I was very clear about the difference. And I was naive to think others were too. But because I was, and because the three-year grant I was working under in Orangeburg was soon to expire, I was susceptible to the phone call I got from Currie McArthur. He was still the superintendent in Sumter, where he'd moved when he left Beaufort. And his district was facing integration. He asked if I'd come help the white and black high schools integrate.

What he really meant was desegregate. He wanted me to put a lid on things, keep things orderly, when Lincoln, the black high school, merged with Edmunds, the white high school. That was his goal for Sumter District 17.

I saw it as a challenge and I accepted it, thinking I could practice what I'd learned in church as a child: that God loves all people and we should too. I thought school boards were ready to abide by the law that was put forth in 1954. Fifteen years had passed; that was enough "deliberate speed" for the South to fully integrate. It was 1968 when the U.S. Department of Health, Education, and Welfare mandated integration.

But it was all a matter of how you understood the meanings of those words, and how far you were willing to go to put those meanings into action. So here is where I'm bowing out of the story, at least my telling it like I have up to now. I'm turning it over to Aïda Rogers, who's been listening to me recall this world I lived in that must seem so strange to her now. It was real, though. It was a real asylum.

There was a barn behind the Newberry, South Carolina, home where Bill spent his early childhood in the 1930s. Cats lived in the barn and he loved to play with them. "I like cats and cats seem to like me," Bill said. Courtesy of the author's collection.

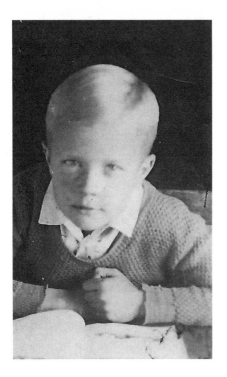

When Bill Dufford was in the second grade at Speers Street Elementary School in Newberry, South Carolina, friends and family gave him the nickname "Cotton" because of his bright blond hair. "You know, I can remember all of my elementary school teachers," Bill said. "My second grade teacher was Annie Abrahams. She was a good teacher. All of them were good." Courtesy of the author's collection.

In 1938, the Duffords gathered in the yard of their home on College Street in Newberry, South Carolina, for a family photograph. "That's when I was twelve years old," Bill said. "I was the baby of the family." Seated, from left to right, are Bill's sister, Doris; his father, C. A. Sr.; his mother, Alma Cole, and Bill. Standing, from left to right, are Bill's sister, Virginia; and his brother, C. A. Jr. Courtesy of the author's collection.

When Bill Dufford was a teenager, he wore his red and white Senior Life Saving badge as a lifeguard at the Margaret Hunter swimming pool in Newberry, South Carolina. "The pool was closed in the mid-1950s when black people showed up to swim," he recalled. The civic pool was filled in with dirt to avoid its integration. Courtesy of the author's collection.

Bill (right) and his older brother, C. A. Dufford Jr., in Newberry in 1945 while they were on leave from their respective military service in the U.S. Navy and the U.S. Army Medical Corps. "We were both on leave," Bill said. "I'm sure my mama was worried. The war was going on and these were her two boys." Courtesy of the author's collection.

Bill Dufford is seated, third from the left, with members of the K-1 radar division on the stern of the cruiser USS *Los Angeles* in 1945. "They were great kids," Bill said of his division members. "They were easy to get along with and compatible. They were from places like New Jersey, Wisconsin, and Pennsylvania. For this kid from Newberry, South Carolina, they gave me a clearer world view." Courtesy of the author's collection.

This photograph of the Port of Shanghai in the 1940s during Bill Dufford's service overseas shows the U.S. Navy being greeted by locals. Courtesy of the author's collection.

Bill is in the front yard of his family home on College Street in Newberry. "It was probably taken about the time I was in college," he said. After finishing his military service in the U.S. Navy, Bill attended Newberry College from 1946 to 1949. Courtesy of the author's collection.

Bill Dufford, then principal of Winyah Junior High School, as he appeared in the school's 1954 yearbook. Courtesy of Georgetown County School District, Georgetown, South Carolina.

This is a 1957 photograph of the Winyah High School varsity basketball team. It was the last team Bill would coach. "It was a great team," Dufford said. "Those boys won about twenty ball games." Courtesy of Georgetown County School District, Georgetown, South Carolina

Bill Dufford was principal of Beaufort High School from 1960 to 1965. This photograph appeared in the school's 1961 yearbook, the *Beaufortonian*. "I don't know where I got that shirt," Bill said, "but I was dressed up that day!" Courtesy of Beaufort County School District, Beaufort, South Carolina.

This photograph of Pat Conroy, senior class president at Beaufort High School in 1963, appeared in the school's yearbook, the *Beaufortonian*. Bill was principal at the time. "Pat had been a student at Beaufort High for one year, his junior year, and in the spring he was elected president of the senior class. That was the story of Pat Conroy. He was so easy to get along with, so accepting. His election also spoke volumes about the other students who accepted him into their fold." Courtesy of Beaufort County School District, Beaufort, South Carolina.

PART 2

1969–1976

AÏDA ROGERS

Chapter 15

⌁

Spring 1969

A WHITE PLYMOUTH SPORT FURY was heading north to Columbia from Orangeburg on U.S. Highway 21. Behind the wheel was a man with a receding hairline and thick sideburns. He was on his way to meet Dr. L. C. McArthur, superintendent of schools in Sumter District 17. They and others in McArthur's administration would then board a plane at the Columbia airport and fly to Washington to meet with officials from the U.S. Department of Health, Education, and Welfare. McArthur and his men had a "final plan for integration" to present to the government.

The man with the sideburns was William Ephraim Dufford, but people call him Bill. Or Dufford. Or now, with his Ed.D. from the University of Florida, Dr. Dufford.

This wasn't the first time Dufford accepted an offer from McArthur. They'd met eleven years earlier, when McArthur taught Dufford at the University of South Carolina in Columbia. Dufford had been a young teacher and coach at the time, not very experienced. McArthur, then superintendent of schools in Beaufort, was richer in experience and advanced degrees, including one from Columbia University in New York. Both had had navy careers—McArthur had won a Bronze Star for action during his four years in World War II. McArthur had kept in touch with Dufford over the years and followed his progress. In 1958 he had offered him a job as principal of Beaufort's new junior high school— Dufford had experience as Georgetown's first junior high principal— and then in 1968, to help him integrate schools in Sumter. Dufford turned McArthur down in 1968. He was still new in his job as director of one of the state's seven Educational Development Staffs. He felt obligated to stay in Orangeburg.

But after the Orangeburg Massacre in February 1968, Dufford was more receptive to McArthur's call. Would he come to Sumter to help them integrate? With nothing more conclusive than a verbal "yes," Dufford drove to Columbia. The trip to Washington was just for a day, to see if HEW officials would accept the plan McArthur and his staff devised.

In an HEW conference room, the Sumter officials rolled out their plans. Dufford was stunned. The plan was to change attendance lines, with Liberty Street determining which students attended which schools. Dufford knew the neighborhoods were divided, that educated whites lived on the north side of Liberty and poor whites and blacks on the south. Standing speechless in the back of the room, he was thinking he should sneak out and tell somebody with HEW what was really going on, that McArthur and his admins were trying to keep the schools segregated. But he didn't have to. After excusing themselves to check their own census data in another office, the HEW people returned and rejected the plan.

It would not work, HEW told the Sumter officials. It would lead to resegregation.

On the quiet plane ride back, Dufford was figuring. Should he take the job? He didn't sign a contract. Maybe he should stay in Orangeburg another year, see what happens, he thought. But then he thought about schools, and how he liked everything about them, and how he had not really worked with kids since he left Beaufort in 1965. Four years was a long time to go without doing what you love.

He decided to accept the job, and the noble challenge of integration. He knew it was the right thing to do: obey the laws of the land, and treat all people equally. The title McArthur gave him was "Coordinator of Secondary Schools." His office would be in Edmunds High, named for a beloved and revered educator, one who left land to be used for Sumter's white schools.

Chapter 16

❧

Welcome to Sumter

A T FORTY-TWO, Bill Dufford knew enough to get the lay of the land before he moved there. Thus his presence in August 1969 at a Ku Klux Klan rally at the Sumter County fairgrounds. Famously the type to never meet a stranger, he was nevertheless a stranger now, witnessing the hate and vitriol he'd seen at Klan rallies in other South Carolina towns.

Dufford wasn't going to let the Klan keep him from the job he had accepted. McArthur had asked him to integrate the schools, and he would to the best of his ability.

One thing he was looking forward to was seeing Reed Swann, his former student from Georgetown. Swann was married now, with two daughters. He'd been teaching and coaching at York High School the past eleven years, putting his broadcast gigs on hold to earn his master's in education administration from Western Carolina University. He'd achieved assistant principal. Dufford had offered him the job of administrative principal at Edmunds, and he had accepted. Ethel Burnett would continue as vice principal, managing guidance and curriculum. Dufford knew her brother, Red Burnett, at Newberry College. In April, Miss Burnett had sent Dufford a friendly, typed letter welcoming him to Edmunds. "Since I shall be the only person remaining of the present administrative staff, I stand ready to accept suggestions and directions concerning anything you want done in preparation for the new year," she wrote. "Please don't hesitate to speak out as you wish."

That was a good sign for Dufford, who was coming up with ways to ease integration between Edmunds, the majority white school, and Lincoln, the completely black school. First on his list was meeting Dr. Earl Vaughn, Lincoln's principal, to see how they could work together. Integration was serious, but that didn't mean the two couldn't be friends. Later in the year, passersby would notice the black and white educators standing together outside Edmunds High, just to get people used to seeing that unexpected pairing. Dufford and Vaughn would go to lunch together, causing heads to turn. And they would conduct meetings together, trying to prepare parents and teachers for the totally integrated schools their children would be attending in the 1970–1971 year.

But in the summer of 1969, Dufford was still in preparation mode. In July, McArthur called a meeting with the top administrators at Edmunds. Noting two of the three were new, he said there were things to discuss so they could "establish a good year." Dufford, Swann, and Burnett joined McArthur in the small conference room next to the former principal's office, where Dufford had ensconced himself.

McArthur immediately focused on Dufford. "The first thing you need to do is get rid of those sideburns," he instructed. Bristling, Dufford pushed back his chair. "Well, if that's all y'all need to worry about over here, I don't need to be here!" He was halfway out of his chair when McArthur backed down, and the meeting resumed.

What followed was conversation that included both a warning and a puzzlement from McArthur. The warning concerned Michael Heriot, a black basketball player who would be returning to Edmunds for his senior year. "He's a troublemaker," McArthur declared. For Dufford and Swann, a red flag waved. How could the superintendent lay blame for all the problems in a school of close to fifteen hundred students on just one person? The puzzlement centered on the black high school students who had attended a summer program at the University of Pittsburgh. They'd returned to Sumter wearing identical caps—all red, green, and black.

"Y'all need to find out what those colors mean," McArthur told the administrative team.

Dufford's ears pricked. It'd be weeks before he learned red, green, and black represented Black Liberation, Black Power, anything to do with people of African descent showing pride in themselves. But he could tell by McArthur's anxiety that colors and symbols were important. They triggered emotion. Dufford started thinking about colors and symbols, and how what they meant could be used to help integrate the schools in Sumter 17.

❧

At the annual pre-school conference at Edmunds High School, Bill Dufford introduced himself to the faculty he would be leading. Edmunds had seventy-two faculty members, ten black, sixty-two white. Freedom of Choice wasn't only for students; black teachers could teach at predominantly white schools as well. At Edmunds, there were 1,461 students enrolled in the school's three grades, tenth through twelfth. Twenty percent of them were black.

Missing at this meeting were two teachers who would always be excused from such meetings: Steve Satterfield, the head football coach and athletics director, and Robert Simmons, the band director. They were with their students, sweating it out on the fields. Football in Sumter, as in many South Carolina towns, was a big deal.

Dufford made a proposal to the faculty. With full integration coming in just over a year, why not show sensitivity to all their students? Football games would be a good place to start. The band could refrain from playing "Dixie," he told them, and the fans could leave their little

Confederate flags at home. Putting a halt to those symbols of white supremacy would make students and parents feel more welcome.

Dufford knew to be diplomatic. The Confederate flag didn't have to disappear entirely. It could be mounted on wall brackets and placed in the rear of the auditorium with the seven flags of countries under which the state had served, as well as the flags of all the countries that had sponsored Edmunds exchange students. With "identifying plates, suitably engraved," these flags could be "flown at assemblies and other appropriate occasions," Dufford wrote in a report later.

As for "Dixie," the key was appropriateness. The song could be played in tribute to those who fought and died bravely, but not when it degraded others and became offensive. Playing "Dixie" when the team scored a touchdown was not considered a tribute.

After minimal discussion, the faculty unanimously approved the proposal. Dufford was pleased, but he knew not to make a big deal out of the changes; that would have provoked unrest. Though later Simmons told Dufford privately that the band would play "Dixie" again, his students no longer played it during the games. And the small Confederate flags fans waved disappeared.

Satterfield, who was coaching two talented blacks on the varsity football team, had no quibble with the changes. Junior C. A. Wilson was a particularly fine player, and it didn't hurt to have him and senior John Pressley, a defensive tackle, psychologically healthy.

Another administrator might have checked with the superintendent or school board before making such dramatic changes. But Dufford, taking full responsibility for his mission, didn't. After the faculty agreed to eliminate the flag and song at football games, he wrote a position paper and presented it to McArthur on August 14. In "The Resolution of a Problem," Dufford outlined the reasons for the changes and the need for people to think in universal, not provincial, terms. He quoted from a 1950 study from one of McArthur's alma maters, Columbia University, stating history shouldn't dictate decisions of intelligent and practical people. Dufford pointed out, in simple terms, that the flag and song mean different things to blacks and whites, and to continue using them "means that we are doomed to conflict and turmoil at our senior high school."

A proposal with unanimous approval was a powerful thing, and because Edmunds High accepted it, Dufford figured other high schools might too. He called the principals of the high schools Edmunds would play that year, requesting that their bands not play "Dixie" when their teams met. It was almost like those principals, facing full integration too, were relieved to oblige. They could tell their band directors they were honoring Edmunds's new policy.

The one exception, Dufford would note ruefully throughout his long life, was Newberry College. When the Edmunds Marching Gamecocks were invited to perform at Newberry College's Band Day, Dufford called president A.G.D. Wiles to request that Newberry's band not play "Dixie." Wiles immediately agreed. He'd been more than firm with the college's white student body in 1966 when Newberry accepted its first black student. "Her name is Nancy Lou Anderson," he'd said at Opening Convocation. "She *is* a student at Newberry College and she *will* graduate from Newberry College. Anybody who has a problem with that should take it up with me."

About fifteen minutes later, Dufford got a call from Newberry's band director. "Why y'all giving in to them damn niggers?" Charlie Pruitt whined. And Newberry's Marching Indians played "Dixie" the day the Edmunds band performed at Setzler Field. It was the only time Sumter students heard it that year.

Chapter 17

⁓

Reunion with Reed Swann

REED SWANN had known Bill Dufford for almost twenty years, and he could tell his old coach and teacher had changed. Not that you could tell it at first. He still whacked boys playfully on the back and boomed out greetings while striding down the halls. He still tended to run late in the mornings. He still knew—in ways his colleagues never could figure—the name of every student in the school. But Bill Dufford had changed, and Swann knew it went deeper than the new sports car and cigars he now favored over the tobacco he once chewed when coaching baseball. Bill Dufford, Swann witnessed in surprise, believed blacks were equal to whites and should be in school together.

Swann was on board with the changes. He'd been questioning the black-white imbalance since his days at Wofford College, where dorm discussions usually ended with participants agreeing blacks had been mistreated and laws needed to change. His mother had been sympathetic to the indignities blacks suffered. During his growing-up years in Georgetown, Willie Mae Swann told her son not to call Martha Smalls "Slop Martha," as others did. Mrs. Smalls made her living selling hogs, and people in town put their leftovers in pails at their back doors for her to pick up for feed. "Miss Willie" Swann always let Mrs. Smalls keep her pails in the basement of her rented duplex, shortening the difficult walk to the pens where the hogs were fed.

As the younger of the two men, Swann wasn't one to argue with Dufford. They'd seen each other in the mid-1950s, when Swann came home from Wofford. Dufford rented an apartment on Frazier Street, near the Swann home on Hazard Street, and it wasn't unusual for Dufford to give students rides. On one particular occasion, the two talked a long time in Dufford's car about blacks, whites, and the differences between them. It had been clear to Swann that Dufford thought blacks were inferior.

In Sumter in 1969, though, Dufford's tune was different. His courting of Dr. Earl Vaughn at Lincoln High and the elimination of "Dixie" and the Confederate flag were just the beginning. More changes were coming. Swann was happy to be a part of it. He'd always been gratified that Martha Smalls had somehow sent all of her children to college. And the $2,000 raise—up from $8,000 per year in York—made it a good move too.

Chapter 18

Student Body President Allen Johnson

S EVENTEEN-YEAR-OLD Allen Johnson knew there was a new man in town. He'd seen the car—white with red interior. Most people in Sumter didn't drive cars like that. He himself had a blue Chevelle, a 1965 model he'd bought with money from his summer job at the city's recreation department. At Birnie Recreation Center, he'd been the only white person in the neighborhood. You didn't have to be on high alert to see the people there didn't have as much as he did, and his own family probably qualified as lower middle class. At the Birnie Rec Center, the basketball goals didn't even have nets.

Johnson learned he needed to be on high alert on at least one occasion. While playing basketball, a young teen pulled a pistol on him. Angry at not having scored, he flashed the gun from the pocket of the pants he wore every day—navy blue Scout pants with gold trim. Johnson was rescued by an older neighborhood teen called Gray Dog, who made sure the boy in the Scout pants didn't come back.

It was a defining incident for Allen Johnson, who grew up respectful of his elders, saying yes ma'am and sir, going to Zoar United Methodist Church in the country every Sunday. Inner-city violence was new. He didn't like it, but after it happened, he realized a bond had been created between him, Gray Dog, and the other young people at Birnie. Black people had been deprived, he realized. They deserved better.

What good fortune for Dr. Bill Dufford that Allen Johnson had been elected president of the Edmunds student council his senior year. Dufford had learned to lean heavily on student council presidents, having them make announcements over the public address system, introduce speakers at assemblies, and take leadership on school and extra-curricular activities. When Dufford invited Johnson into his office at the first of the school year, he quickly found someone he could work with to integrate Edmunds and Lincoln.

Of course, Johnson was interested in other things. He liked girls, and he really liked baseball, and he even liked music, singing in the school chorus. He thought he might like to go to college after graduation, especially if he could get a baseball scholarship. No one in his family had gone to college, and though his father wasn't keen about it, his mother thought it was a good idea. For now, he'd concentrate on his schoolwork, baseball, and trying to pass math.

It wasn't long before Dufford and Swann came to him with an idea they'd been tossing around. Music could be a way to bring students together. Could Johnson and others on the student council organize live "concerts" on campus? Different kids were playing music in garages around town; they'd be welcome to play during lunch outside on Fridays. Johnson lined it up. Soon, curious blacks and whites would gather around a wooden bandstand near the football practice field, listening to whatever the bands, including black performers, played—soul, country, beach, rock and roll. Students who typically didn't interact found they were listening to some of the same music. Every now and then the students would dance.

Allen Johnson was out there too. He liked the music. But baseball he loved. He dreamed of playing professional ball.

Chapter 19

∾

Steps to Togetherness

Though less than one mile apart, Lincoln and Edmunds might as well have been light years away from each other. Both had full academic, athletic, and music programs. But they were as separate as could be. When Bill Dufford and Earl Vaughn began bringing their teachers and students together in 1969 to prepare them for full integration the next year, some of the whites confessed they didn't even know where Lincoln was.

Complicating matters were the names of the schools. In the segregated South, black schools never took the names of their towns. So Edmunds, the white school, was considered "Sumter High School" by the rest of the state. Cheerleaders and baseball players wore a big "S" on their uniforms. Basketball players wore "Sumter" and "Edmunds" on theirs. The scoreboard at Memorial Stadium, where Edmunds played football, said "Sumter." Sportswriters outside Sumter called the school Sumter as well. There was no question that "Sumter" and "Edmunds" were interchangeable.

But in the spring of 1969, the all-white board of education decided to change "Lincoln" to "Sumter." It was their way, Dufford believed, of easing the blow for the white students who'd be going there in a little over a year, in the fall of 1970. White students at a school named for a president who believed blacks were equal? Not in the Jim Crow South.

After the plan to change attendance zones didn't pass HEW, an earlier plan was put back in place. To accommodate such a large student body—two thousand students between both schools—the integrated high school would operate on two campuses beginning in the fall of

1970. Lincoln (the new Sumter) would be for tenth graders only at its Council Street campus. Edmunds, for grades eleven and twelve, would continue at the Haynsworth Street campus. The ninth graders would remain in the district's three junior highs. Dufford and Vaughn, with no blueprint to guide them, began hatching ideas for a smooth transition. But getting people to call it Sumter High School instead of Lincoln was beyond their abilities. Generations of students and alumni couldn't change in one summer.

Still, the Edmunds *Hi-News* obliged. And its earnest, truth-driven staff reported how Dufford and Vaughn brought the two student councils together for the first time on October 24, 1969. The young leaders met at the newly named Council Street Sumter High, where they compared their differing election policies and discussed improving school spirit. The Edmunds group found their counterparts very engaged in school life: they were planning Student Council Week, during which students taught classes, Sumter City Council paid a visit, a Miss Student Council was elected, and a dance was presented. The Edmunds group had financial concerns that semester: with only four home football games, there wasn't much opportunity to sell items to fund activities. The meeting occurred without incident, and Vaughn invited the Edmunds students to come back for a tour. Tom Page, the sophomore class president, told the *Hi-News* he thought the school was "pretty nice" and that "the people are just like the people over here."

Not surprisingly, though, even the *Hi-News* editors—as well as the editors of the *Hi-Ways* yearbook—were confused about Dufford's job title. Maybe it was because he'd moved into the former principal's office, or because "Coordinator of Secondary Schools" was a mouthful. Probably it was because he was the final decision maker at Edmunds and the idea of hiring a new employee to integrate schools was a foreign concept. Either way, students liked his style—casual, open, and firm. Plus, he said the students were mature enough to decide their own dress code, and he gave seniors the privilege to leave campus for lunch. Compared to the previous, more military administration, Dufford was a refreshing change.

His task, though, was huge. Edmunds, with 1,461 students in the fall of 1969, was one of the largest high schools in the state. Even with three grades it was a 4A school, with an impressive roster of athletic teams, arts programs, and clubs. And he knew Lincoln, which had earned its own fine reputation since it opened as an elementary school in 1874, had thousands of former students who didn't want to see it overcome by a wealthier white school. Still, the Lincoln alumni wanted better for their children. Some of their best—and bravest—were already at Edmunds High and Alice Drive and McLaurin Middle Schools as Freedom of Choice students. Decades later, some of their white classmates would admit, ashamed, that they were mean to them in those earlier years.

∾

Like schools everywhere, Edmunds and Lincoln reflected their communities. Perhaps the biggest influence was Shaw Air Force Base. Edmunds in the 1969–1970 school year had a dozen ROTC flights, or units, for boys. "Angel Flights" were for junior and senior girls; their responsibilities included performing at football games and helping with the annual Cadet Ball each fall. Almost every flight had at least one black member, sometimes two or three. With about 350 ROTC student members and four adult commanders, uniforms were common in the classrooms and halls of Edmunds High, mandated attire on Thursdays.

There had been some attempt to help black students feel welcome. A Black Heritage Club had been organized. During the 1969–1970 school year it had seventy-seven members, three of them white. Kay McDowell, the club's "Sweetheart," was black. Michael Heriot was a member; his good friend Norbert Briggs was club president. Bill Dufford had signed on as one of the new advisors; he joined Eleanor Robinson, a black English teacher. Among their objectives was to "explore the cultural heritage of the Black Man before the discovering of America" and "promote better understanding between the races." The Purplettes, a girls precision drill team that took its name from Edmunds's purple and white colors, included seven black members. (Their uniforms bore a prominent "E.") Betty Davis was the sole black player on the girls basketball team, and Bennie Colclough the only black on the boys cross country team. Colclough and six other black students were on the forty-six-member track team. There were no black golf or tennis players—boys or girls. Nor were there any black baseball players, black members of the May Court, or black cheerleaders.

Cheerleaders, Dufford figured, could be one way to help with integration. He decided to send the Edmunds squad to Lincoln for pep rallies. Dufford knew there was a deeper meaning behind the trip than bolstering school spirit. Sending white girls to a black school flew in the face of traditional racist thought—that black boys would attack white girls. Instead, the Edmunds cheerleaders came back enthusiastic from the high energy of a Lincoln pep rally. At a subsequent Lincoln rally, the cheerleaders were late coming back, prompting Edmunds officials to launch a search. They learned the girls were so enthralled by Lincoln's band that they followed them to their band room and listened to them play.

The spirit was reciprocated a few months later when Lincoln's pep band played at the annual Edmunds Holiday Invitational Basketball Tournament.

Dufford and Vaughn made sure the growing relationship extended to faculty, organizing meetings so teachers could plan curricula for the following year. When there weren't enough students at Edmunds to make a driver's education class, those few students were sent to Lincoln to be merged with the class there. Dufford and Vaughn coordinated their school schedules so classes would meet at similar times.

Working through his student council president as much as he could, Dufford had Allen Johnson invite the minister at St. James United Methodist Church, an African American congregation downtown, to deliver the invocation at a home football game. Later, Dufford was invited to speak at St. James. It was the home church of C. A. Wilson, who was having a really good year in football. And it was the only church Dufford was invited to attend in Sumter that year.

Chapter 20

☙

Breaking the Ice in the Hot Tub

IF SCHOOLS REFLECT THEIR COMMUNITIES, they also reflect the times. At Edmunds, Bill Dufford and Reed Swann knew things were a lot different from their days together as teacher and student in Georgetown. A sense of innocence marked their recollections of those postwar years, but they felt no innocence in 1969. America was at war in Vietnam. Some students at Edmunds didn't believe in it, and wore black armbands to school in solidarity with the peace movement.

"Hippies" were a new group of people. They frequented a weekly "coffee house" organized by a Sumter church; their presence was debated in the Edmunds *Hi-News*. A visceral fear of the Soviet Union, communism, and nuclear war got mixed with the idea that somehow blacks were at the root of those fears. Sumter District 17 even offered a semester course in communism. *Hi-News* editor Susan Bryan, the valedictorian, went after several institutions in print. "Racism Is Ancient Relic" headlined one opinion piece. In another, "Who's a Child," she examined lowering the voting age to eighteen while excoriating the adults in Lamar who turned over buses carrying young black children to school. Scholastic press contests earned her ire for limiting entries to school-related stories. The *Hi-News* famously covered shocking poverty "Within a Mile of Edmunds," revealing a family with children who didn't know how to eat with utensils. It also championed the adult education course at Lincoln, where a Sumter mother of eight had earned her diploma.

Women, too, were changing. Students still wore plaid skirts, but high above the knee instead of comfortably below. At Edmunds, juniors Patricia Brewington and Gwen Padget did the unthinkable— they drove school buses. For one black student, Brenda Holmes, riding the school bus was "simply deplorable," but not because of the drivers: in a letter to the *Hi-News*, she wrote white students wouldn't sit with her. Meanwhile, the home economics department invited boys to take "Bachelor Living," a males-only course that would focus on "personality development," home management, and garment mending. It was a time of transition, a peculiar time when a student could be honored as a Betty Crocker Homemaker of Tomorrow at the same time as "Age of Aquarius" could be chosen as the theme for the Miss Sumter pageant.

Leighton Cubbage had gotten past all that. A junior lineman, he'd had his epiphany the year before. There he'd been with his white self in the locker room whirlpool with C. A. Wilson, the star black player on their J. V. football team. Both were nursing leg injuries. They'd been having a terrific year, one with no losses. They'd even beaten the varsity in a scrimmage and been written up in the newspaper.

Not knowing Wilson really well but finding himself in tight surroundings—and naked except for jockstraps—Cubbage searched for something to say. Finally, he stammered out something about how they were both having a good season and asked Wilson how it was going for him. Wilson agreed, and their eyes met. "It sure is different from last year," he said, "when everybody was chasing me around the school yard and calling me 'nigger.'"

It was a moment, a comment, that would change Cubbage forever. He would remember the cold October night, the window open, the sound of the team practicing outside. He would remember looking at his white skin and Wilson's black skin, shining in the water of the locker room whirlpool. And years later, a successful businessman, he'd publicly affirm his belief that people should look at others as individuals, not groups. He'd say he learned that as an athlete at Edmunds. Bill Dufford was the first adult he saw who put that belief into practice.

Chapter 21

❧

For God and Coach

S TEVE SATTERFIELD had an epiphany too. Unlike Leighton Cubbage, though, he had prayed for his.

"Lord," he'd prayed from the library of Appalachian State University, where he was working on a master's in secondary education so he could get a raise, "I can't work any harder. What's wrong with me?"

And, as Satterfield told the story, the Lord replied. "What in the hell do you mean? You get them up at 6:30 in the morning for a meeting and if they're late you give them hell. If the lines on the practice field aren't straight you give the guy hell. You want everything to be perfect and we've only had one perfect person in the history of mankind."

Satterfield, who was teaching five English classes as well as shouldering the duties of head coach and athletics director at Edmunds, was told to change his method. "Have FUN," God thundered. "Give up. You don't care if the lines aren't straight, you don't care if there aren't helmets, you don't care if the manager's got the footballs out there. Quit having all these meetings and doing all this stuff that is counterproductive."

Decades later, Satterfield would joke that being from Greer, he didn't know what "counterproductive" meant. But he got the message. He decided to lighten up on his players and himself. "Fun" had become an almost forgotten concept to Satterfield, who'd unwittingly fallen into Edmunds's strict administrative culture in the nine years he'd been there. Teachers were admonished to keep their desks straight. Students were to stay in straight lines, whether for lunch or for buses. Punctuality was imperative. Henry Jackson, the former principal, could famously shout for thronging students to fall silent in the halls. Satterfield had toed the Edmunds line and was making sure his students did the same.

It was understandable that Coach, the second son of a street preacher who built a Baptist church with a handful of recovering alcoholics, would take his burden to God in that spring of 1969. The fall of 1968 had been his only losing season. The Edmunds varsity Gamecocks had lost seven games, won three, and tied one. Even the J. V. team had, as the phrase went, "whomped 'em upside the head." His experienced players had graduated, and he'd be working with a new batch of boys. Quarterback Jimmy Eaves had never played that position. But he'd employ his new "fun fundamentals," as he'd been divinely instructed. There wasn't much to lose.

Then came two signs as the 1969 season began: senior linebacker Jordy Johnson told him they'd win every game, and Bill Dufford arrived. Dufford took two of Satterfield's English classes off his back and had no interest in the neatness of teachers' desks. Satterfield felt himself relaxing. At the game against Hartsville he told his players if they weren't having fun, to come out of the game. In the pouring rain, the Gamecocks slipped, slid, and beat the number 10-ranked Red Foxes 27–0. It was the second game of the season, Satterfield's best. The Gamecocks would win every game that fall, taking the Region III championship and beating Gaffney for the state title. For Coach, who'd quarterbacked against Gaffney in his high school years, Edmunds's 22–15 victory was made particularly sweet by defensive tackle John Pressley's courageous play. Warning him that Gaffney played rough, Satterfield advised him he could go the easy way and step aside when their two running backs tried to score, or take a sprinter's stance and hit the first guy in the nose. Pressley chose the latter and won Edmunds's Most Hustle Award that year.

Oh, there was no question to Steve Satterfield that "Fun" was a good idea. Dufford had given him freedom to pursue it. His wife could think "the new Steve" was crazy all she wanted, but he knew the Lord had sent him a man who was okay with his philosophy.

Chapter 22

❦

The Salvation of Walter McRackan

To WALTER MCRACKAN, there was no question what he was, and he could sum it up in one word: trapped. Sumter in 1969 was no place for a curious tenth grader. He knew there was a world out there, one that could teach him more than he was learning at Edmunds. He'd said as much to Bill Dufford, who'd called him in for a discussion about why he kept cutting school. McRackan had been blunt: the soap operas he'd been watching at home were a lot more interesting than the classes at school. Though the term wasn't in vogue yet, Walter McRackan was showing signs of being an "at-risk" kid.

He'd been trying to make life as bearable as possible. He was a member of the Esquires, a boys social club that had parties in an abandoned sharecropper's shack in a field down a country road. Its counterpart, the Les Rois—French for "the Kings"—did the same in another. Alcohol flowed at those parties, consumed by those of age and younger than the legal eighteen for beer and twenty-one for liquor. For members, the smell of marijuana smoke was becoming familiar, and LSD, courtesy of the teens with ties to Shaw Air Force Base, made an occasional showing. McRackan, in his khakis and oxford cloth shirts, stayed away from the drugs. But underage drinking was nothing new to him.

Edmunds was a big school, and like many tenth graders, McRackan was just another student lost in the mix. He wasn't a jock, he wasn't in student government, and clubs weren't for him. He was in the ROTC, but otherwise his habit was to come to school just enough to get a passing grade and to hang out in the smokers section during lunch. For that privilege all he needed to do was what the other kids did, forge his parents' permission. They both worked, making it easy to fake going to school only to come back home and tune in *As the World Turns*.

But Dufford was keeping an eye on him and his friend Johnny Hirschberg. When they'd gotten caught smoking with some other friends in the bathroom, Johnny had put his cigarette out in Dufford's coffee. Truant as McRackan was, he never would have done that. Johnny was sent swiftly to Reed Swann, who handled discipline.

McRackan was watching Dufford too, taking in his style of management by circulating, and he noticed how it created a lighthearted, friendly atmosphere. No student would have had the nerve to put out a cigarette the way Hirschberg did before Dufford arrived. McRackan was figuring out what others had—that Dufford took an interest in all students, not just the Beta Club kids and the star athletes.

That interest didn't stop after those students graduated. Years later, when McRackan was in college, Dufford would drive Hirschberg to see him in Durham. He wanted McRackan to talk to his old friend about how he could rebuild his life after some bad decisions. McRackan wasn't surprised. "Dufford always had a penchant for the lost lamb."

Chapter 23

Ɑ⌣

Bus Ride

BILL DUFFORD AND EARL VAUGHN were conferring. They knew they needed to do more to bring their black and white students together. As weeks went by and integration came closer, they devised more intense interactions between Edmunds and Lincoln. Pep band and cheerleader visits were a start, and joint student council meetings were great. But something more profound was required. Dufford and Vaughn decided a group of students from Edmunds needed to be brought to Lincoln for a semester-long class.

It was a risky idea. Most white parents wouldn't want their kids going to a black school. Dufford looked to his student council president, Allen Johnson, to lead the way.

"You know my daddy's not going to go along with that," Johnson told Dufford. Edwin Johnson was a white man of his time, a man with an eighth-grade education. He worked at the phone company and his wife, Rachel, worked at the Campbell Soup Company. Edwin had grown up on a farm and made sure there was a good-size vegetable garden at his house as an adult. His five kids could work in the garden, and they could go to work after graduating from high school. Edwin

Johnson, like his son, was friendly and industrious. But he didn't think the races should mix.

"Let me take care of Edwin," Dufford assured him, and he made plans to drive to the Johnson's small home on Wilkie Street. As he had before, Dufford stayed for supper. Rachel Johnson was a talented and hospitable cook, and she and Edwin were impressed with Dufford, so personable and well-spoken. At the kitchen table, Dufford told the Johnsons that integration was unavoidable and their son, as the school's leader, was the best candidate to help the process succeed. Dufford knew that if Allen Johnson were allowed to take the class at Lincoln, other students would follow.

Allen Johnson held his breath. He didn't know what his parents— particularly his father—would say. Edwin was one to let loose with the N word.

He needn't have worried. His parents readily agreed. In a few weeks he'd be anxious again. It was time for the bus ride to Lincoln.

༄

The first day of the second semester, about a dozen white students boarded a school bus at Edmunds, bound for their American Government and Communism class at Lincoln. The five-minute journey seemed much longer to the silent, anxious group. When they entered Lincoln's double doors, the scene that unfolded crystallized itself in Allen Johnson's memory. "Everybody stood back. All the blacks backed up against the wall."

The Edmunds students had shared classrooms and gym space with black students for years. But this was the first time they were the minority. The experience was one Johnson would appreciate for the rest of his life. He would have nothing but praise for Fannie Ivey, the unflappable teacher who treated her black and white students equally, and the black students he befriended in her class.

"They were okay with us being there," he recalled. "I was sitting there thinking, 'They're taking the same classes we are.' I really enjoyed being there."

The rest of the semester, the bus rides to and from Edmunds didn't seem so long.

Chapter 24

ᕙᕗ

Scuffle

IN RETROSPECT, there was a sense of Camelot about the "Dufford
Year" at Edmunds High. The football team's state championship
would be remembered as the greatest feat by many, but there were
plenty of other remarkable achievements. The Distributive Education
Club, the state chapter of the year for the second year in a row, would
travel to Detroit to compete in the national contest and win it. The
Hi-News would win the David A. Tillinghast Memorial Award for
"effective leadership in South Carolina scholastic newspapers" from
the Southern Interscholastic Press Association, which also bestowed
honors on *Signature*, the school's literary magazine, and *Hi-Ways*, the
annual. The Edmunds newspaper won the state's 4A paper of the year;
the *Gamecock Show* broadcast program took top state honors from the
South Carolina Scholastic Press Association as well. The Marching
Gamecocks won second place in the state's 4A band competition and
performed in a pregame show at the Gator Bowl in Florida. Dufford
was one of the band's chaperones. The *Hi-News* reported he presented
a discussion about sex and teens based on the Kinsey Report.

For many athletes, though, the Dufford Year would be their glory
year. The cross country team won the state championship, its second
consecutive one; the track team lost only one meet on their way to
winning the regional championship. The baseball team, with Allen
Johnson on the mound, took second place in the regional. Even the
tennis team, which finished fourth that year, enjoyed a much better
season than usual.

The boys varsity basketball team also enjoyed success, making it to
the finals of the lower state championship. The team's Most Valuable
Player was Michael Heriot, its only black member, whom School
Superintendent L. C. McArthur had labeled a troublemaker.

Dufford had run interference for the talented guard. Heriot, he
believed, had been mistreated for years by the whites he'd gone to school
with, and wasn't one to not defend himself. One night after a game,
white adults had called out criticisms of his playing. Heriot barked back.
Tensions and voices rose outside the Edmunds gym. Dufford, knowing

white adults wouldn't criticize white students in public, had ushered him away.

But one morning at school Dufford showed more solidarity with Heriot, mainly because Heriot had shown solidarity with a white student who was also being bullied. Senior Michael Wehunt, a major in Flight A of the Junior ROTC, began chastising sophomore Joe Cutter, an enlisted member of Flight H. Cutter was a small boy from humble means in an ill-fitting uniform. His pants drooped. That was reason enough for the upperclassman and ROTC officer to begin his verbal assault.

Witnessing the abuse, in the halls when classes were changing, was Michael Heriot. He told Wehunt to get off Cutter's back. A scuffle ensued between Heriot and Wehunt, severe enough for alarmed teachers to send for Dufford. It didn't take long for him to get the story and figure out what to do. Wehunt and Heriot were suspended for the rest of the day—Wehunt for harassing a student, Heriot for interfering in ROTC, and both for fighting. Dufford, knowing Heriot would have to walk a long way to get home, offered him a ride. Wanting a chance to talk to the youth, Dufford pulled into the Holiday Inn.

Sipping coffee at a table in the hotel restaurant, Dufford became aware of a group of local white businessmen at another table. Their gestures and facial expressions told him what he suspected—a black student with a white educator was an unwelcome surprise. Heriot, Dufford realized, was so used to the reaction he didn't seem to notice.

Later, Dufford would hear from Superintendent McArthur. Wehunt's father had called, and McArthur wanted a written report of the incident. Irritated, Dufford remembered a similar situation in Beaufort, when McArthur had requested a report after a student's father had complained. The student's father should have come to him, Dufford believed, and furthermore, McArthur should have stood up for his administrator. The whole thing was beginning to give him a sour taste.

Chapter 25

❦

Parents Speak Out

A s MUCH AS EDMUNDS HIGH HAD GOING FOR IT, it was obviously lacking one thing—a decent gym. Poorly lighted, the bare-bones gym had subpar locker rooms and little space behind its basketball goals. Teams, coaches, cheerleaders, and fans were cramped. Parking was bad.

Steve Satterfield was well aware of the problem. But he saw a solution. The new Bates Middle School was almost complete. It had a spacious gym and well-lighted, paved parking. As athletics director, he asked Bill Dufford if the Region III tournament, which Edmunds had been chosen to host, could be played there.

There was one catch, and both men knew it. Bates was on Estate Street, in the middle of a black neighborhood. Dufford, recognizing an opportunity to prepare for integration, decided to go forward with Satterfield's idea.

At practice that afternoon, Dufford and Coach Boykin, the boys varsity basketball coach, told the players and staff about the change in venue. All were in agreement that the Bates gym was the best choice for the tournament. That afternoon, Dufford got a call from Mrs. O. V. Player, whose son Spencer, a senior and Dufford's stalwart third-period office helper, was on the team. "Who made that decision?" she asked. "I did," Dufford responded, unwilling for Satterfield to take the heat for what he knew could become a struggle. He explained their thinking to Mrs. Player.

Shortly after, the phone rang again. A disapproving L. C. McArthur was on the line. Dufford realized what he hoped to avoid had now come to pass, Mrs. O. V. Player's husband was on the school board. O. V. Player had called McArthur.

"You can't move the tournament," McArthur told Dufford.

Again, Dufford went through the reasoning. "Let me talk to the board," he offered. "I'll lay this thing out with some sensibility."

McArthur agreed, but he needn't have. When Dufford made his case before the board, he was a deer caught in the headlights. The board decided the tournament would be at Edmunds, and the board had the last word. Defeated in this effort, Dufford realized that when it came to integration, students were much more reasonable than their parents.

Chapter 26

༄

Alabama Kisses

A S DUFFORD BEGAN LOSING POPULARITY with the Sumter 17 school board, he was gaining favor with organizations about which he was unaware. One was the Center for Integrated Education (CIE), a division of the University of South Carolina's College of Education, whose mission was to help South Carolina's public schools successfully integrate. Coach Steve Satterfield had attended one of the CIE's "small group" meetings and came back impressed. "You need to look into this group," he told Dufford.

From seemingly out of the blue, the Southern Leadership Conference in Atlanta sent Dufford an invitation to bring his students to Alabama, where race riots were raging. The idea was for some Edmunds students, black and white alike, to share their experiences and strategies for integration with students in Tuscaloosa. Dufford, Reed Swann, and Ethel Burnett conferred about which students to send.

One, naturally, was Allen Johnson. It would be his first plane trip, and possibly, he would recall years later, his first trip out of the state. Leighton Cubbage, a student council representative as well as a football player, also was chosen. So was sophomore Barney Shorter, who played J. V. football and basketball, and Susan Bryan, the crusading newspaper editor. They and others, with Dufford, Swann, and Moses Rabb, a psychologist and small group expert with the CIE, made the trip.

It was one of those events that wouldn't take on importance until years later. Rabb remembered Allen Johnson as a natural leader, making friendly conversation on the plane with black and white students. Cubbage remembered how, when he got to the room in Tuscaloosa where they would meet the Alabama students, he kept his eye out for good-looking girls. Dufford remembered how important it was to him,

Swann, and Vaughn that the meetings be student-to-student, with as little adult interference as possible, based on their success in Sumter with this same approach to peer-to-peer resolution.

He realized, more than forty years later, that the work he and his compatriots had done in Sumter was monumentally more progressive than almost all other places in the state. Violence and political maneuvering in Calhoun, Dorchester, Orangeburg, and York Counties in the late 1960s and 1970s were described in detail by USC history doctoral candidate Luci Vaden in her 2014 dissertation. The Alabama invitation was proof that the higher-ups thought Sumter was a model other schools could follow.

What Dufford did know at the time was that Alabama was having a harder time integrating—with all race issues—than South Carolina. It was a truth made most clear to the Edmunds students when one of their white Alabama peers asked, in pure, innocent confusion, "How do you do it? How do you integrate?"

After some silence, Leighton Cubbage came forth with an answer. "It's like the first time you kiss a girl," he said. "You just close your eyes and do it."

Chapter 27

◠◡

Pool in School

B ILL DUFFORD wasn't the only Edmunds educator concerned about students who weren't achieving. Coach Steve Satterfield was too. So was Eddie Weldon, the school's assistant football coach, head golf coach, and guidance counselor. Weldon had a talent Dufford was taught to shun in his youth: he was a pool shark. And he'd discovered some of his lowest-achieving students—all boys—were exceptional pool players.

Weldon and Satterfield conferred. Wouldn't it be nice if those boys could get some solid mentoring in an environment in which they felt comfortable? Could a second-floor lobby in the school auditorium be transformed into a place where Weldon could use his professional guidance and recreational skills to help those boys? Dufford and Swann weren't hard to convince. Getting a pool table up a flight of stairs wasn't easy, though. Several strong boys were enlisted for the job.

By mid-spring, Room 217 was taking shape, and with more than a pool table. There was a ping-pong table, a jukebox, and a foosball table. Students could spend their lunch hour or study hall there, provided they had a pass. Two student council members would supervise Edmunds's "Recreation Room and Lounge." It was a far different space from the former ROTC headquarters, and black and white students could be found there.

"It gave us an opportunity to hang out," Allen Johnson would reflect, "and our school kind of became the cool place to be."

While students were finding more reasons to come to school, Satterfield, in a sense, was falling in love with his career. This was the way he wanted to teach. This was the way he wanted to coach. With Dufford's permission, he revamped his English classroom. Gone were the hard wooden desks in straight lines. In their place were easy chairs in a circle. To him, good learning could only happen in comfort. If a kid needed to sleep, he would let him.

Satterfield also had fallen in love with a book. Harper Lee's *To Kill a Mockingbird* spoke to him with its message of racial justice and compassion for all God's creatures. He assigned it in class. Many of his students balked. *To Kill a Mockingbird*, with thirty-one chapters, was too long, they said. Undeterred, Satterfield got hold of several paperback copies.

"Read just this chapter and come back to me tomorrow," he said, ripping out chapter 1. It worked. Soon, students came back wanting more than just the next chapter. But Satterfield stuck to his one-chapter-a-day strategy, tearing out pages until all that was left were covers. Former administrators wouldn't have okayed such a practice, but under Bill Dufford, Satterfield's creativity flourished.

To help prepare for full integration, Satterfield taught one of his classes at Lincoln. The class included sixteen students from both schools—all boys, all potential dropouts. When Dufford asked Satterfield to teach those students how to write, he pondered a method. Finally, he told his students to take out a piece of paper.

"Write down your passion," he instructed, "and it can be only one word."

Of the sixteen passions that emerged, the one that surprised Satterfield most was "goats." He read the word out loud.

"How can goats be the number one thing in your life?" he asked the boy.

"Coach, I can't explain it to you. You're going to have to come and let me show you my goats."

Satterfield went to the student's family farm that afternoon, where he watched a herd of goats come up and lick the boy, who fed them, hugged them, and excitedly told his teacher all he knew about his animals. The next day in class, he told his students to write everything they knew about their passions, and not to worry about nouns, verbs, or anything except getting their words on paper.

For the next few weeks, Satterfield spent ten minutes a day with each student, going over their papers until they had them right. He presented the goat paper to Dufford, who read it dumbfounded. "I didn't know you were teaching a college prep class," he said.

"I'm not," Satterfield said. "You gave me these guys."

"These guys" were typical for Dufford to notice. Satterfield knew Dufford was trying to find a program that would work for the district's lowest 10 percent. He was with him all the way.

Chapter 28

༄

Becoming Familiar with the Unfamiliar

As THE DAYS lengthened and the school year began drawing to an end, Bill Dufford knew more needed to be done to bring Sumter's blacks and whites together. On May 5, 1970, he sent a letter to the parents of District 17's current ninth graders, who would be leaving their three junior high schools for tenth grade in one place. That place would be Lincoln High, now referred to as Sumter High. Edmunds High would accommodate eleventh and twelfth graders.

They began referring to the two schools by their addresses. Lincoln/Sumter High was the Council Street campus, and Edmunds High was the Haynsworth Street campus. Full integration meant the Haynsworth

Street campus school would be a "unitary senior high school" for 1970–1971, Dufford's letter informed.

The letter also stated that the current ninth graders would attend an orientation at both campuses during one of three days in May, during which plans for their high school future would be discussed. Parents would be invited to "an explanatory session" in "the near future."

In short, parents and students—black and white—needed to become familiar with schools with which they'd been unfamiliar. And Dufford knew it sure would help if there was one name for that "unitary senior high school."

He and Earl Vaughn discussed the matter. Full integration was at their doorstep, and more and more parents were opting to send their children to Sumter's two private schools next year. They decided to ask their student leaders to lead. The two student councils had been meeting throughout the year; *they* could decide three very important things: the name of the unitary senior high school, its colors, and its mascot.

The student councils gathered one afternoon in the Lincoln High library, sitting across from each other at tables. Vaughn and Dufford gave them their charge and left the room. Discussions began.

In less than an hour the three decisions were made. The senior high school would be named Sumter High. Students agreed that the district's senior high school should be named for the town it was in. Its mascot would remain the gamecock. In a town named for General Thomas Sumter, the "fighting gamecock" of the American Revolution, nothing else made sense, they concurred. The colors? Goodbye Edmunds purple and white. Edmunds won the mascot; it was only fair for Lincoln to retain its royal blue and gold. Decisions that might have taken months for a board of elected officials to make were handled easily by a group of teens.

Dufford thought the decisions made sense, not that he would have interfered with the compromise. He knew the next step was for the students—not him—to make the announcement. Allen Johnson, president of the Edmunds student council, and Walter Isaac, president of the Lincoln/Sumter student council, would present their decision to the board of trustees. Dufford attended the board meeting.

After some silence, the board thanked Isaac and Johnson, and asked Dufford to leave the meeting while they discussed matters. Dufford headed to the porch downstairs. About a half-hour later, he was called back. Nothing was mentioned, but he couldn't help but think the board wasn't receptive to the students' decisions. It was a victory for the students and for progress, but one of reluctant acceptance on the part of the board.

Chapter 29

❧

On the Steps of Edmunds Gym

THOUGH IN NEED OF REPAIR, the Edmunds High School gym was a critical place on campus. Its outdoor lobby area was where students gathered each morning, socializing on or around the steps before the bell rang and the doors opened for homeroom.

One morning before school, a black girl made a comment about a white girl's fashionable outfit. The daughter of parents who owned a clothing store, the white girl was always well turned out. She took offense at the comment and brought the matter to Vice Principal Ethel Burnett, who took it to Swann, who took it to Dufford. The girl didn't know who her black insulter was. Like with many white students at Edmunds, to her all blacks looked alike.

It took Swann a few days of detective work to identify the black girl. Dufford and Swann decided they'd ask her to apologize to the white girl. An apology would be sufficient, they figured, and the matter would be settled.

Dufford, Swann, and the two girls met in Dufford's office. The black girl apologized.

"Is that enough for you?" Dufford asked the white girl.

"No," she huffed. "I want something *done* to her."

Shocked, Dufford decided on a measure that would bring the least chaos. He told the black girl he would have to suspend her. Satisfied, the white girl left. Then Dufford told the black girl she wasn't suspended, and could carry on with her day at school.

The decision reflected Dufford's "under the radar" way of helping people get along and keeping things running smoothly. There was no way the white girl would know the black girl wasn't really suspended: Dufford knew she wouldn't be able to recognize the black girl from any other.

The news about how Edmunds was preparing for integration had spread to North Carolina, something the administration learned when about fifteen students from two historically black colleges arrived unexpectedly one day in early spring. It was spring break for the North Carolina Agricultural and Technical State College in Greensboro and Johnson C. Smith University in Charlotte, the students explained. They'd heard good things about Edmunds; could they observe classes? Permission was granted, with the condition that if they caused any disturbances they'd have to leave. They knew the visit wasn't authorized by the colleges.

Of the two schools, A&T had earned national recognition for civil rights activism. In February 1960, four of its students "sat in" at the all-white Woolworth's counter, prompting fame for "The Greensboro Four."

On this day in 1970, the college students behaved as requested. But as classes changed and afternoon approached, administrators became aware they were participating in discussions and causing some disturbance. True to their word, administrators told the North Carolina students to leave, sending Edmunds student helpers to guide them down the halls to the exit.

The college students gathered quietly across Haynsworth Street in an area between a fenced backyard and the sidewalk. They stayed there, making no move to leave.

Dufford and Swann decided not to get rattled, and not to call the police, something many administrators would have done. They came out of their offices and sat on the steps leading to the gym, across from the students. Nobody said anything. Tension was high. Dufford pulled out his fingernail clippers and started clipping. Thirty minutes passed.

Then, the students drifted off.

"It was almost like a showdown, but nothing ever happened," Allen Johnson would recall.

And Dufford would recall never knowing how the students were traveling. He never saw their cars. But he did know that staying calm was best. It made things easier than getting emotional.

Chapter 30

ᠭᡍ

Good Luck Class of 1970

VOLUME 34, NUMBER 12, of the *Hi-News*, issued May 29, 1970, covered many end-of-year topics. "Good Luck Class of 1970" ran at the top of the front page, and a small exam schedule was placed at the bottom. The caption under a photograph of formally dressed students on a dance floor informed readers that "An Evening in Venice" was the theme of the junior-senior prom, and that sophomores served refreshments to the upperclassmen in the school gym. "Teachers Depart; Cheerleaders Named" was the headline for a two-column story.

Bill Dufford was most concerned about graduation. He'd learned that several students had been chosen to speak, but few of them were African American. The newly diverse student population wouldn't be adequately represented with only white student speakers. He took the matter to Grady Locklear, head of the English department. Locklear acted as a sort of Edmunds editor, reading over scripts and speeches the public would hear.

Locklear told Dufford a student committee had chosen the speakers; Dufford asked if he could talk to the committee. Locklear agreed, and Dufford outlined his reasoning to the students. The next year all the black students from Lincoln would be at Edmunds—the "new" Sumter High, he told them. Fairness dictated that more black students speak at graduation, reflective of the student body. The students agreed.

The upper administration accepted that several selected black students would speak at graduation, but before they did, Dufford had to write a two-page paper explaining why having black speakers was important. He was definitely getting the picture that McArthur really wasn't as interested in integration—true integration—as he was just managing a difficult situation of mandated desegregation, a meaningful distinction for Dufford then and still today.

ᠭᡍ

There was no doubt Allen Johnson was having a good year. The baseball team had done well, and he'd been named Most Valuable Player. He'd won the lead male role in the spring musical, *The Pajama Game*. He'd been a delegate to Boys State, was voted "Best All Around" by his class-mates, and he'd passed math.

As president of the student council, he'd been given responsibili-ties. A favorite was introducing guest speakers and performers at student assemblies. Allen Johnson never forgot meeting Lieutenant Clebe McClary, a former student of Bill Dufford's in Georgetown. McClary had come out of Vietnam the year before without an arm and an eye. But, resplendent in his U.S. Marine Corps uniform, he stood when Johnson walked into Dufford's office.

"He respected me, just because I was the student body president," Johnson marveled years later. "Nobody ever did that."

Dufford had asked Johnson to invite McClary to speak to the students at Edmunds High, and he'd done so. "There were fifteen hundred students and teachers and administrators there, and when he spoke, not one person didn't weep that day."

Dufford also asked Johnson to invite the Swordsmen, a Columbia gospel quartet. Johnson thought many of his classmates wouldn't be receptive to a religious program, but he was surprised. Edmunds, after all, had a Bible club—103 members strong—that met weekly for devo-tions and discussion. Johnson was a member himself.

Yes, it had been a good year. He'd give his speech, "The Nebulae," at graduation. After that, it was anybody's guess. His father wanted him to get a job, but he was wondering how he could get a baseball schol-arship and go to college. His mother thought it was a good idea. But nobody in his immediate family had gone to college, and getting there was a mystery.

Chapter 31

෴

Pomp and Circumstance

THOUGH SUMMER had not yet officially arrived, June 1, 1970, in Sumter, South Carolina, was searingly hot. Those assembled that Monday at Memorial Stadium would remember the heat. The Sumter climatologist reported an 87-degree high, and it felt much hotter in a football field with no shade. On such a scorcher, the last class of Edmunds High School would rehearse for graduation.

Bill Dufford was there. So was Superintendent Currie McArthur and Fred Welles, the board's business manager. Instructions were given about how the students would process to and from their seats on the field. Then each student was to walk across the front row of their chairs to receive their diplomas, shake hands with McArthur, Dufford, and Welles, and return to their seats.

The theme for Graduation Day was "One World but a Million Stars," and the student speeches were titled to reflect that theme. All went well until it was time for the students to shake Currie McArthur's hand. Michael Heriot, McArthur's "troublemaker," didn't. Nor did John Pressley, the football standout who'd won a scholarship to Presbyterian College. Charles "Chuck" Heyward, a track team member and *Hi-News* staffer, was the third senior who didn't shake McArthur's hand.

McArthur stopped the practice and stepped to the microphone. He announced that some of the students weren't shaking his hand, and that shaking the superintendent's hand was required to graduate from a public school in South Carolina. In the broiling heat, McArthur and Fred Wells, the board's business manager, moved aside to study the state Department of Education's code of regulations, searching for the language confirming that shaking hands was mandatory. After several minutes McArthur resumed the rehearsal. But, he said first, the students in question would need to sign a paper stating they would shake his hand at graduation. They could do so in the office of the coordinator of secondary schools. That was Bill Dufford.

Taken aback by McArthur's reaction and subsequent order, Dufford received the students in his office later that day. In hindsight, Dufford would berate himself for not checking with the South Carolina Department of Education about whether McArthur's handshake declaration was true. He would ruminate that McArthur figured he, Dufford, would try to talk the students into shaking his hand, and graduation would go smoothly.

Dufford did neither. He told them to do what they needed to do. Heriot came forth to say he'd sign a paper. Heyward and Pressley did the same. Dufford took the paper to Superintendent McArthur. But at the actual graduation exercises that evening, the trio would not shake hands with McArthur. It was a turning point for many in Memorial Stadium.

The *Sumter Daily Item* reported the incident on the front page of its June 2, 1970, issue: "Dr. McArthur stopped the ceremonies at this point and explained to the audience that as a representative of the state of South Carolina and under the laws of this state he could not grant a diploma to a student who failed to show proper respect to state and national institutions."

The article didn't carry a byline or name the students in question, but someone got the following quote from McArthur the morning after graduation: "A handshake is part of that institution, and a failure to shake hands was a failure to acknowledge the state."

Bill Dufford would be angry for decades that McArthur had called those students "criminals," and he promised that he would get their diplomas back.

"It showed courage on the part of those kids not to shake his hand," Dufford would say. He wanted an apology for Heriot, Heyward, and Pressley. For his part, McArthur wanted evidence from the Department of Education's code of regulations, language he had not been able to find during the graduation rehearsal, that supported his stance. McArthur asked school board attorney Shepard "Shep" Nash, with Nash and Chappell in Sumter, to produce evidence that made clear a mandate that students must shake hands with the school superintendent as a state and district representative in order to graduate. What Shep Nash provided instead was a brief letter, just three sentences, dated June 17, 1970:

Dear Dr. McArthur:

I have considered the matter of withholding diplomas from the three colored students, who refused to shake hands with you on graduation. There is grave doubt in my mind, that the School has any legal, enforceable right to maintain a successful suit against these young people. I would certainly not advise that the school trustees attempt to take legal action in the matter.

Nash's legal opinion to McArthur was never reported locally. No diplomas were returned. No apologies were issued, even to this day, and justice for Heriot, Heyward, and Pressley—wrongly branded as criminals—went unserved. While those students were able to move on in their respective paths—including Pressley's acceptance of his awarded scholarship to Presbyterian College—without any legal ramifications, the episode still weighs heavily on Dufford's mind as a transgression by those in power against those with a right to protest that power.

Chapter 32

☙

The Biggest Achievement of the Year

W HEN THE APOLOGY NEVER CAME, Dufford knew his efforts to integrate successfully were going to seed. It was obvious he wasn't seeing eye-to-eye with the upper administration and school board, rendering him powerless. He needed to leave Sumter 17.

He wasn't the only one coming to that recognition. Reed Swann had put in his notice. His mother-in-law in York was sick, and his wife wanted to be home to help care for her. York High, where he'd worked eleven years, offered him the position of assistant superintendent when he called to check on openings. Swann knew the work he and Dufford were doing was doomed.

There was no question Sumter had been affected by what happened at Memorial Stadium the night of June 1. The executive board of Local 273 of the United Furniture Workers of America, members of the AFL-CIO, met on the evening of June 3 to discuss the "handshaking incident." The group, composed mostly of African American workers, passed a "Resolution on Compulsory Handshaking." It stated, "The custom of 'shaking hands' is a meaningful ritual only if it expresses a feeling of 'good will,' mutually shared, and if it is a forced ritual and the implied 'good will' does not exist, for whatever reason, then the ritual of 'shaking hands' is a lie and a meaningless hypocrisy." The Local 273 executive board didn't hold back in their resolution's conclusion:

THEREFORE BE IT RESOLVED:

1. That Superintendent McArthur is condemned for insisting that certain students "shake hands" with him as a condition for receiving their diplomas.

2. That Superintendent McArthur is condemned for any implication that refusing to "shake hands" with him should cast any shadow of a criminal act or criminal intent upon any person so refusing.

3. That Superintendent McArthur is condemned for needlessly escalating their refusal or failure to "shake hands" and by so doing has demonstrated a lack of self control and "good judgement" which

may seriously jeopardize the future development of an integrated public school system in this area which will serve to advance the interest of people of all races.

The *Sumter Daily Item* covered the meeting, reporting it in the June 4 issue.

Two days after Local 273 met, the Sumter Committee of Concerned Parents (SCOCP) printed and distributed "A Statement Concerning the Issues Related to The Edmunds High School Graduation Incident and Profiles of the Three Black Boys Whose Diplomas Were Invalidated by Dr. McArthur." The four-page document described the incident as the SCOCP, an African American group, saw it:

> We do not know why Dr. McArthur decided to attack these young men so maliciously with his actions and his tongue. In fact, we were shocked to see the Superintendent of our school district demonstrate such narrow-mindedness in handling the situation. Those of us who were at the stadium saw a sour side of Dr. McArthur last Monday night. He seemed vicious as he snatched the diploma from Mike Heriot and as he publicly denounced Mike's friend, Chuck Heyward, for removing Mike's diploma from the podium. Our shock turned to shame as Dr. McArthur continued to insult us by attempting to cloak his illegal and uncouth actions behind a veil of "disloyalty to the State of South Carolina and its institutions."

The SCOCP pointed out that students shook Dr. Dufford's hand, proving that they weren't rebelling against "The Establishment," as students in colleges and high schools were that year nationwide. Nor were they "raisin' hell" just for the sake of raising hell. Rather, their behavior can be traced to something of a more serious nature." The document continued:

> These kids wanted badly to graduate. For four years they had bravely endured the tensions associated with being a part of the Black minority in a school system that was desegregating for the first time. They were anxious to unload the burdens that they had had to carry as the community's chosen representatives to make school integration work in Sumter. Yes, they really wanted to get their diplomas, so much so that some of them actually cried when they finally realized how helpless they were to make an expression

of free speech during the final activity of high school. Many of us cried too. Some cursed, but others cried.

The SCOCP noted that Chuck Heyward's father had come from Hampton, Virginia, to see his son graduate, and Michael Heriot's aunt had traveled from Bishopville. The Pressley family was there in force, "proudly expecting to see their diligent son who had never been a disciplinary problem in school, accept his diploma."

The truth is that these Black students are not hoodlums or troublemakers. They come from good families. They are scholarly in their school work, and they all have leadership abilities. We must not stifle the potentially good qualities in these youngsters. Neither can we sit back and allow an insensitive administrator to push them up against a wall and eventually drive them into criminal channels. We must encourage that which is good in them, support them when they are right, and thank them for having endured whatever suffering they might have experienced from Sumter's painful experience of integrating its school system, as is legally required by the U.S. Government.

What followed next in the document were individual profiles of Heriot, Heyward, and Pressley, describing their personalities, achievements, and families. Pressley was praised as "an able student whose versatility is his great virtue." Along with talents as a comic, school radio broadcaster, bus driver, and football player, Pressley was called "well-disciplined," "quite articulate," and "mature in his actions." Noting that his father was "a shop foreman at a local industry," the group concluded "Sumter should be proud of John Pressley."

After describing Heyward as a "quick-thinking, good looking, Afro-coiffed boy who has also braved three years of minority experiences at Edmunds," the group wrote this: "It is easy for a powerful administrator who is unable or unwilling to understand the frustrations and aspirations of Black people to crush Charles' hopes, shatter his dreams, and disillusion him forever. We need able, willing, administrators to give direction and inspiration to determined, alert Black youths such as Charles. Charles has maintained a good high school record and has been accepted at a good college to continue his education. We must do something to see that Charles is able to continue to seek his goals. We must not let the actions of an impulsive superintendent ruin this Black youngster's future. Charles needs his diploma. He deserves it. He has worked hard for it. His parents have made many sacrifices for it."

The profile of Michael Heriot was last. "Mike is a born leader," the profile started. "Someday he will be a great man." The group pointed out his courage at Edmunds, instances of suspensions when he stood up for the rights and dignity of African Americans.

> Mike says, "So often people, especially Black people, want change; but they are afraid to initiate change." He continues, "Do you know I was once suspended because I got up and in a dignified manner, walked out of an assembly where they were bringing in the Confederate Flag and I didn't want to witness it? My friend Norbert was threatened with suspension because a white kid told the principal that he thought Norbert had spit on the Confederate Flag."

Heriot's college plans were discussed, his good academic scores, and his athletic prowess and awards. In its conclusion, the SCOCP paraphrased a line from "Yet Do I Marvel" by Harlem Renaissance poet Countee Cullen:

> Why did Dr. McArthur see fit to unjustly punish and embarrass these young people the way he did? We won't attempt to say why, for we know not what "awful power compels his awful mind." But it is obvious that Dr. McArthur is not the kind of broadminded, intelligent educator we need to lead the Sumter community during these times of racial tension.

Dufford and McArthur were clearly not of the same mind on this issue. For Dufford, a call to continue his good work in more receptive environs came, and he could not refuse the opportunity. The people at the Center for Integrated Education, who had been watching Dufford's work from its station at the University of South Carolina in Columbia, offered him a job as field services director, which he accepted.

But Sumter had been the most challenging work of his career, and leaving was hard. He'd built lasting friendships with Earl Vaughn, Ethel Burnett, Steve Satterfield, and others. It was hard to leave them, and the students too.

He didn't officially resign until July, which gave him time to compose an end of year report. Within its five pages Dufford summarized what was done and what happened to help Sumter 17 prepare for a unitary school in 1970–1971. He included things that didn't happen that were happening elsewhere in the state, namely cuttings and knifings, phoned-in bomb threats, classroom walkouts, picketing, and cherry bombs in restrooms. Vandalism of school property at Edmunds was the lowest in years, he noted. Not having those kinds of disturbances created a "wholesome environment" in which students could better learn.

"Quite an unusual thing occurred," he wrote, "when in March of 1970 the Edmunds faculty invited the presidents and registrars from all colleges or universities in South Carolina to the Edmunds campus. This resulted in the 'Establishment of Dialogue' when 20 colleges were represented. Some good possibilities for the future dictate the pursuit of this dialogue."

It seems Bill Dufford's abundant people skills had served the district well: he had started a parent discussion group, he had promoted an in-school "availability committee" to which minority students could take grievances instead of going outside the school for support, and he had helped teachers start viewing conditions "as good or bad and not as black and white."

Dufford also stated what he thought was the biggest achievement of the year: "the advance in human understandings among students." As he put it, "There was developed the beginning of a healthy respect for one another as a person and understanding for those who are different. Admittedly, this was only in the beginning stage but progress was evident."

The *Sumter Daily Item* published an edited version Dufford's report, and news of his resignation got out fast. Anna McDonald, a black guidance counselor at Edmunds, read about it at USC's Capstone House in Columbia, where she was a General Electric Fellow. She sent him a two-page, handwritten letter expressing her sorrow and shock.

"Even now, it just does not seem possible in this year of 1970, that a man could be so crucified because he is humane—and this is what everything is all about in spite of many other things that may be said," she wrote, adding that she remembered hearing rumors that he may leave and that she and Dufford even discussed that possibility before the end of the school year. "Because of you and Mr. Swann and Miss Burnette, this past year to me was an unforgettable one. … the thing that you instilled in your assistants was fairness to everyone and since I did not know you prior to last year, I could not know to expect the depth of your feeling concerning this—and this is what made everything so unforgettable! Also, for the first time in the many years that I have been teaching, I felt that I was a part of progress—of change—because of you."

When she read about his resignation, McDonald wrote that she experienced "a flash of awareness that I was lost in this world in dire need of protection and no protector was there—no one to stretch a helping hand. What can we hope for without you, Dr. Dufford?"

❧

After the graduation spectacle, Bill Dufford knew without a doubt he and Currie McArthur couldn't work together. They thought too differently. Still, Dufford could appreciate McArthur's intellectual gifts and what he'd done for young black children in Sumter in the mid-1960s. His preschool program was nationally recognized; when Dufford had been director of the Educational Development Staff in Orangeburg, he'd had educators in his district visit Sumter to learn more about it.

But McArthur differed from Dufford on one insurmountable point: Dufford thought McArthur believed the races should be separated. "He could do things for black people as long as they stayed over there. His preschool program was well done and well-staffed. But his definition of desegregation was to do something for them, but 'don't you bring them over to sit with me.'"

Dufford held the opposite view, and between the two men it was an irreconcilable difference, one made all the more evident in the vast difference between the progress made in Sumter during Dufford's time there and the backsliding that would follow his departure.

Chapter 33

❧

Baseball Dreams

AFTER GRADUATION, Allen Johnson was at loose ends. A lot of his friends were going to college, but his future was unsettled. At five foot ten and 165 pounds, he was a lot smaller than what scouts were looking for. Still, Memphis State had called. And so had Wingate—not that he knew what or where it was. He did know he had a friend there, and it had a baseball team.

In 1970 Wingate was a junior college outside Charlotte. The baseball coach invited him to come up and throw. On a field of knee-high grass, Johnson took the pitcher's mound and threw to his friend. The coach offered a half-scholarship for one year—$750—more than they had ever offered a baseball player in the program's history.

It was good news and it was bad news. Johnson was elated by the offer, but he knew the family budget couldn't cover the other $750. He told Wingate he'd have to come up with the money and to let him see what he could do. He figured he might have to forego college and get the job his father kept talking about.

At home on Wilkie Street, he told his parents about the half-scholarship. Rachel Johnson overrode her husband, Edwin. "We'll have to try to work something out," she said.

Bill Dufford, at home on Burkett Drive, knew his student had been to Wingate. He invited Johnson to come tell him about it. Johnson drove over and repeated what he'd told his parents. Johnson told Dufford he didn't know if he could accept Wingate's offer because $750 was more than he could afford. "I don't know what to do," he concluded.

Dufford pulled out his checkbook. At his kitchen counter he wrote Allen Johnson a check for $750. What Dufford said next Johnson would carry the rest of his life: "Pay me back when you can and if you can, and if you can't, the hell with it."

Allen Johnson completed his two years at Wingate and then won a full scholarship to USC. He paid Bill Dufford back the summer after his freshman year, laying sewage pipe for a construction company.

Edwin Johnson helped his son move to college that summer of 1970. Allen Johnson found out later that his dad cried on the way back home.

Chapter 34

⌒⌀

Left Behind

IN HER LETTER TO BILL DUFFORD, Anna McDonald put into words what others in Sumter 17 were thinking.

"What the next year will bring for any of us, those left in Sumter on you leaving, concern me greatly," McDonald wrote. "For us left behind, I can see little because our leader will be gone."

Walter McRackan didn't want to see Dufford go. During the school year, he'd gotten close to him, Reed Swann, and Ethel Burnett. The ultra-bored, on-the-verge-of-dropping-out sophomore was becoming a more involved junior.

Something else besides Dufford's interest in him had affected McRackan. In January, a group of students from Morris College, a historically black college in Sumter, tried to enter the town's First Presbyterian Church. McRackan had been across the street, buying snacks from a vending machine in the interim between Sunday school and services. He watched as leaders of the church in which he'd been baptized told the black students to leave. The police arrived and arrests were made. McRackan, who believed and agreed with the adults who'd preached that blacks were inferior to whites, was sickened.

"Even a racist can't turn somebody away from church, for gosh sakes," he would later say.

That day at lunch, he announced he wasn't going back to First Presbyterian Church. His mother, a devout Christian and public school teacher, agreed, but with the caveat that he attend church somewhere. McRackan agreed. The next Sunday he went to Alice Drive Baptist Church with a friend. He was shocked when the congregation voted to follow the same procedure as First Presbyterian, should the Morris College students try to enter.

McRackan eventually found a home at an Episcopalian church that had a black member in the choir. On January 24, the *New York Times* ran a story about the January 11 incident and McRackan learned it wasn't the first time Morris students had tried to worship at a white church and been turned away.

Feelings of disappointment and shock about white churches weren't new to Bill Dufford. But Walter McRackan, consciously or not, was waking up. He admired Dufford, and he wasn't going to lose touch with him. Columbia was only about fifty miles from Sumter.

Chapter 35

∽

Freedom Song

It's likely no group of citizens in Sumter 17 appreciated Bill Dufford more than its black high school students. They sent him a letter after he resigned with a quote from Dr. Martin Luther King Jr. at the top: "We must live together as brothers or perish together as fools."

"Dear Doc," it started:

We (black students) feel that the above words of the late Dr. Martin Luther King pretty well describes the goal that you, working along with us, have tried to reach this past year not only at the two high schools but in the community, the goal of living together as brothers.

We feel that one can truthfully say that there has been a mutual sharing and acceptance of each others likes and differences because we have been open with one another. "Openness," as Grace Elliot wrote, "is the key to the discovery of all of life."

May you continue to prosper, maintain your <u>rare</u> ability to be open, and when you come to some (<u>another!</u> (smile)) crisis in valuing your ideas on race relations, just think of the words of "Lift Every Voice" that goes "Stoney the road we trod ... " But never forget the words of our own favorite freedom song in the NAACP that says, "Don't let <u>nobody</u> turn you 'round!!"

Keep in touch and May God be with you always.

To: You

From: All of Us

The letter was also signed by the bishop of the local AME church, indicative of the community support behind this message from the students. If Bill Dufford had doubts about his work during his one year in Sumter, the letter from the black students erased them for good.

Chapter 36

❧

Summer Upheaval

VICE PRINCIPAL ETHEL BURNETT composed a short, handwritten note to her supervisor. She dated it July 3, 1970. "Dr. Dufford," she began,

> If you're not here when I get back, I'll write to you. In the meantime you have my very deep personal appreciation for your fine qualities as a human being and a humanitarian, my professional appreciation for what I've learned in working with you, and my admiration for having retained balance and good humor when all about you were over reacting.
>
> There'll be no forgetting—and there could be something of your philosophy and spirit left here that won't die. I'll work to that end.
>
> E.

Ethel Burnett might not have been at Edmunds that summer of 1970, but Dill Gamble was. As assistant principal at Lincoln, he'd moved from Council Street to Haynsworth Street with Principal Earl Vaughn, where the two would resume their roles when full integration began that fall. Also, Gamble was running District 17's summer school program. He had to be at Edmunds.

But things started feeling not quite right when he saw James Stover move into an office in the same building. Stover had been principal at Lincoln before Vaughn, and was back after a few years in Florida.

Gamble didn't know Stover would be returning, and couldn't figure out what his position would be. With rumors flying about Bill Dufford leaving and Reed Swann already gone, Gamble figured he needed to know where he stood. He stepped into Currie McArthur's office to find out.

"He stood up angrily and said, 'You will never teach in this district again, you will never coach in this district again, you will never be an assistant principal, you will never be a principal in this district again,'" Gamble remembered years later. It would take years for him to piece together how he and McArthur had come to that fiery moment. Gamble had marched in downtown Sumter earlier in the 1960s. He and other Lincoln educators, including Leo Twiggs, Lincoln's first art teacher, protested that Sumter business owners weren't hiring African Americans. Gamble received a three-page, single-spaced letter from McArthur the Monday after the Saturday demonstration. "The last paragraph said, 'I don't expect to see any of my teachers back downtown demonstrating.'" Gamble marched the following Saturday.

Then, during the 1969–1970 school year, as Sumter 17 prepared for integration, Gamble and McArthur found themselves in the same sensitivity session. Managed by USC's Center for Integrated Education, the session required each member to ask a question of another. Gamble chose McArthur. "Why is it so difficult for you to answer a simple question?" McArthur, Gamble remembered, never really did answer his question, but after the session McArthur had a question for Gamble.

"He asked me what I thought of him as an administrator," Gamble recalled. "I said I had a great respect for him as a leader, with the exception of when it comes to integration. He became very provoked. He said, 'Now I know how to staff my schools.'"

The relevance of that sequence of run-ins became clear to Gamble later. But late in the summer of 1970, after the meeting with McArthur, he considered himself fired. It was a huge blow for someone who'd hungered and fought for his education, who didn't know what a library was until he was in tenth grade, who, as an airman first class in the Air Force, turned down scholarships from UCLA, the University of Michigan, the University of Oregon, and the Air Force Academy to attend Morris College in Sumter, where his high school girlfriend had won a scholarship. With one week of summer school to go, Dill Gamble packed up his office, made sure payments were made, told his secretary he'd been dismissed, and went home to Azalee Bates Gamble, the girlfriend he married when he returned to South Carolina from Korea and the Philippines. He told her they'd have to sell the house they'd built in 1962.

Azalee was calm. She told her husband they weren't going anywhere, that her teaching job would keep them going. She suggested he call some friends. They might know of some jobs that might suit him.

Gamble listened to his wife, and less than a week after the confrontation with McArthur he had a job with the Center for Integrated Education. He'd be commuting from Sumter to Columbia, working on the campus of a university that didn't accept African American master's degree students when he and Azalee had been working for theirs just five years earlier. No, they had to go to North Carolina College in Durham for his in history and hers in elementary education.

But that master's degree—and earlier board approval of his job as assistant principal of the newly named Sumter High—apparently meant little to Superintendent McArthur. Gamble had lost the job he loved so much. Not only had he advanced to assistant principal from social studies teacher, head track coach, and assistant football and basketball coach, but he'd done it at one of the best black high schools in the state. With its library and foreign language department, Lincoln High in Sumter was worlds away from Melina High in Sardinia, where he'd grown up, and St. Mark's in Williamsburg County, where he'd taught his first year.

Dill Gamble liked Sumter. He liked living there and working there, and while he knew District 17 had problems, he still thought it was a good system. Getting fired stung.

Chapter 37

☙

A Statewide Mission

IN HINDSIGHT, it almost seems as if the decades-long working partnership between Bill Dufford and Moses Rabb was meant to be. Though they'd met during the Edmunds trip to Tuscaloosa, the two would forge a lasting friendship at USC's Center for Integrated Education. Rabb, a black psychologist from Rock Hill, could match Dufford's extroverted personality. And he recognized that Dufford's "explosiveness" and connections with administrators statewide was what he and his colleagues at the CIE needed to help South Carolina's public schools integrate.

"We needed someone who had guts," Rabb recalled. "We needed someone who had conviction and was strong enough to implement it, speak about it, and do something. Dufford was the guy to do it."

Funded by a federal grant, the CIE's practice was to go into districts only when invited. Many times they weren't. Several districts had severe difficulties and violence had occurred, with perhaps the most famous being the March 1970 incident of about two hundred white parents turning over two school buses of black children going to a newly integrated elementary school in Lamar. More minor incidents prompted invitations—usually fights between black and white students. Rare was the invitation to help board members or administrators, the decision makers whose actions would have lasting effects.

One such occasion did arise in Kershaw County, however. The superintendent asked for help with his integrated staff. There was a sense of mistrust between them, Francis Addy Snelgrove said.

Following policy, Dufford and Rabb—one white, one black—drove to Camden to facilitate talks and solutions. The educators gathered in a circle.

Dufford could tell the races weren't communicating. Techniques he and Rabb tried to get them to talk failed. Dufford suggested that the blacks meet in one room and the whites in another. That way people, no matter their color, would at least feel free to talk among themselves. Then both groups could reconvene and hear from both facilitators the concerns of each group, and then try to work through their problems.

Snelgrove nixed the idea. "That's separating people again," he said.

Dufford reasoned nobody would talk if there was no trust between the two groups, but the superintendent wasn't swayed. "They ran me out of the meeting," Dufford recalled. "We were sitting there and could have stayed three days waiting for them to be honest about their concerns."

Jasper County also called on the CIE, but for more than just its schools. Leaders wanted help with city and county councils too. The CIE's staff wasn't big enough to handle such a large assignment, and Dufford thought his former student Pat Conroy might be able to lend a hand. Conroy was teaching on Daufuskie Island, one of only a few white people on the island. Dufford knew Conroy was forming friendships with his students and their families, and thought he'd make a good facilitator for the small group discussions the CIE was planning.

As Conroy wrote in *The Water Is Wide*, he accepted his former principal's offer after asking permission from his supervisor, another teacher. With her permission, he took a week off from work to help Jasper County leaders in Hardeeville. A week later, back on Daufuskie, he was fired because the board said he violated district policy by not getting "proper" permission. Conroy would never be a professional teacher again.

"But he did follow policy," Dufford would say. "He assumed his immediate superior took it up the line. He was being railroaded, it was obvious. If the true story be known, he got fired because he was educating young black students and because he was a consultant with the CIE at the request of Bill Dufford."

Moses Rabb was with Dufford and Conroy in Jasper County, and he quickly realized the needs there went far deeper than integrating schools, already majority-black. Institutional racism and historic poverty resulted in an overwhelming number of poorly prepared teachers. "It was so bad we held classes at night in reading, writing, and arithmetic—not just for people in adult ed; we had them for teachers. We had mostly teachers. We found these people couldn't read or write. I know they had degrees, but I don't know where they got them."

Not all teachers in the county were so underprepared, but there were enough for Rabb to see the poverty and the absence of a good education perpetuating themselves. "One of the reasons districts were so poor was they couldn't afford to hire teachers who were better prepared." In Jasper, most of the black teachers would have been categorized as B or C teachers according to their National Teacher Examination scores. It didn't get by him—Dufford either—that the district superintendent sent his children to the all-white private school with more resources than were available in the district's public schools.

One other dramatic thing happened during the CIE's time in Jasper County. Dufford and his colleagues realized they were being followed back to their cars after meetings. It seemed even though leaders of the county wanted their help, others weren't quite as enthusiastic.

∿

The CIE was under the direction of USC's College of Education. As in the greater world, not everybody in the college was in favor of integration. And not everyone in Dufford's life knew he favored integration.

One of his former players, coaching at Columbia's Eau Claire High School—then mostly white—invited him to a meeting at the school. A group was gathering. "You'll like it," the coach told Dufford. But Dufford was appalled when he heard Cecil Tucker, a USC education department chair, describe how integration would diminish educational opportunities for white students. Mooney Player, a revered white football coach at Lower Richland High School, also spoke, warning against black athletes. Later Player would claim Hayes Mizell, an outspoken integrationist and school board member, took public buses because he was an alcoholic and couldn't drive.

Dufford thought the group was destructive. Black head coaches, he knew, were usually a casualty of integration.

Hayes Mizell, Mooney Player, and Deadline '72

Bill Dufford wasn't the only outspoken white man working for fair integration in the 1960s and 1970s in South Carolina. M. Hayes Mizell was doing the same. As director of the South Carolina Community Relations Program of the American Friends Service Committee, Mizell's job was to facilitate school desegregation in the state. One way he tried to accomplish that difficult mission was to get elected to the Richland District 1 Board of Trustees in 1970. His advocacy for integration and fairness for poor African Americans brought him a reputation as a "liberal," enough to make him a target of those who wanted to maintain the status quo.

Installed on the board in January 1971, Mizell was entering treacherous waters. In July 1970 a group of white adults called the Concerned Parents Association had begun organizing in Columbia. At a meeting at Eau Claire High School, parents talked about not being able to afford private schools after integration. In notes Mizell kept, one woman said she planned to send her children to live outside the district "so they don't have to go to a nigger school." A man said, "We can stop this communist conspiracy."

Two weeks after the meeting, a flyer circulated with this headline:

UNITE AND WIN
I LOVE MY CHILDREN
DO YOU LOVE YOURS?

The paper included this passage:

This dreadful thing must not be allowed. Are you going to stand by, complacently, and let our school system be set back a hundred years?

Are we going to let the morals of our children be jepordised [sic] by idiots from another part of the country, where nothing like this change is in effect, nor is there likely to be in the future.

We have long been the scapegoats for the political aspirations of every bunch of morons that dream up these stupid changes. We must not wait to change back. We must stop the change before it is made.

The flyer concluded by asking readers to vote for write-in candidates in November, to contact their congressmen and senators, and to come to the next meeting in August. Its final encouragement was to "Help send Mizell home."

The Concerned Parents Association wasn't able to keep Mizell from winning the board seat, but a more organized effort was launched two years later. Five of the seven board seats were open, and a group named Deadline '72 aimed to fill them with conservative members who thought as they did. Ostensibly named for the 1972 election, "Deadline '72" really meant the 1972 election represented the last chance to "save the public school system" from full integration, Mizell said. Its main organizer and spokesperson, Coach Mooney Player, told the *State* newspaper its goal was to end the "permissiveness of the school board ... and take control of the board from Hayes Mizell."

The athletics director at Lower Richland High School and a renowned football coach, Player had been involved in the earlier Concerned Parents Association. And he'd been written up from 1969 through 1971 for physically abusing African American students at Lower Richland. In one instance, charges were filed against him and he was fined in magistrate court. Still, in April 1972 he told the *State* he wanted more African Americans to join Deadline '72. "We need more blacks in the group, and we won't do it if we offend them with racial generalities."

Deadline '72 accomplished its goal. At the November 1972 election, all five of the group's candidates—all white men, all Republicans—won the panel of seats by a nine thousand-vote margin. Among the defeated candidates were three incumbents: Lincoln Jenkins, an African American lawyer, white farmer Sam E. McGregor, and white farmer Robert Lee Scarborough, who'd served twenty-four years, sometimes as chair.

Also defeated was Mizell's friend and comrade Dr. Robert J. Moore. The head of Columbia College's history department, Moore had worked on civil rights issues. His candidacy had been singled out by Deadline '72. "If Deadline '72 has one goal, it will be to defeat Moore for the school Board," Player said at a press conference, covered by the *State*. "We are dead opposed to Moore because we can't stand another Mizell on the school board." For his part, Moore responded that he'd never met Player and was shocked by the happenings.

A record $13,300 was spent on the Deadline '72 campaign; the victors promised to work for a "restoration of quality education" when they took office. They also favored "stronger discipline, the neighborhood school concept with as little busing as possible to bring about racial balance and a broadened academic program with more vocational schools, honors programs and general business courses."

Mizell, who criticized the term "quality education" as vague and dubious, wasn't up for election in 1972. During the next two years, he and Dr. Shepard Dunn, the other Democrat on the board, would learn to work with the five new Republicans. Deadline '72 didn't exactly attain its goal: the five new members weren't always able to overpower Mizell. The reality was, as the members got to know each other and work together, they learned Mizell wasn't "the anti-Christ" they'd thought, as Dunn told him.

"Even those Republicans, when we were serving, came to see I was not wild-eyed," Mizell recalled. "When they got to know me, they realized I was a person to the left of them. I cared about the schools and about things working. And as it turned out, those Republicans did not all think alike or have the same temperament, so they had some differences of opinion among them."

Still, Mizell was defeated in 1974, then reelected in 1982. Observing his travails and triumphs was Bill Dufford, who had endured his own fires in the fight for fairness. Their missions brought them together, and intersected via David Abel, who worked in Mizell's office and managed the Summer Study program Dufford advised in 1971. Dufford was incensed when a Columbia newspaper quoted Player theorizing that Mizell had a drinking problem because he took a public bus from his home to work in downtown Columbia. "I knew I had an ally in him and he knew he had an ally in me," Dufford said. "We were working for the same purpose but at different levels."

True indeed. In his position with the American Friends Service Committee, Mizell was his own man. There was no board to abide by, no supervision. Dufford, by contrast, frequently was constrained by bureaucracy, a board, and a that's-the-way-we've-always-done-it mentality. Through the hard times, both men could usually maintain their humor. Mizell recalled a fun little gift Abel and Dufford brought him when the Deadline '72 group was working. That gift is in Mizell's extensive archives at the South Caroliniana Library at the University of South Carolina: a jockstrap with a piece of satin sewn on it, inscribed with "Scratch Deadline 72" in glittery letters.

Chapter 38

⌒

Sumter Fall-Out

WHILE BILL DUFFORD was working with schools across the state, Walter McRackan was watching what was going on at the "new" Sumter High. With Dufford, Swann, and the previous class of standout athletes and scholars gone, the school seemed to sag. A campus that once buzzed with activity after the final bell seemed quiet. The bands that played during lunch the year before were silenced. School dances ceased. The junior-senior prom was cancelled. The militaristic atmosphere that existed before the Dufford Year returned, and Coach Steve Satterfield began looking for a job.

It took just a few months for him to find one, and by the time he announced he was leaving, both campuses of Sumter High experienced unrest. Other African American educators left, and the black members of the basketball team boycotted. When it was announced Satterfield's position would be filled by a white assistant coach instead of a black one, the African American students at the Council Street and Haynsworth campuses protested. During one particularly difficult incident, Dill Gamble was asked to visit students who'd been jailed. Still chafing from his dismissal from Sumter 17 several months earlier, he nevertheless agreed to see the students after his commute from Columbia. There he was shocked by what he saw: injured teens who hadn't received medical care. He also was angered by what he heard: McArthur had called a special assembly only for the black students, during which he gave them instructions for the proper way to behave. "Hell, excuse me," Gamble reflected years later. "What about *all* of the students? That within itself would provoke students: 'What have we done? Why have we been called out of our class while our fellow white students are getting their lessons? What have we done to listen to you telling us how to behave?'"

The students decided to return to their classes, Gamble was told, and when McArthur tried to stop them at the doors, those upset and angry black students pushed past him. The police were called and students were arrested, but no newspaper reports captured the full scope of this incident, in keeping with what historian Walter Edgar has described as a "conspiracy of silence" on the part of southern newspapers of the era.

Later, the *Item* would report that the superintendent suffered a fractured rib. That was only one detail in a long, tangled, and emotional string of incidents in which students were suspended or expelled, meetings were held, hearings were scheduled, and accounting was made for a riot in which windows were broken and restrooms were destroyed. It was a scar for the district, and Gamble, unable and unwilling to get emotionally involved, purposefully didn't. He stuck to his duties with the CIE in Columbia.

Still, it was jarring to see young people suffering in jail, and he offered comfort as best he could. The wardens were concerned too. "They said the kids were okay—to the extent they still had dried blood and weren't dead."

～

As the school year progressed, junior Walter McRackan's focus veered in an unexpected direction. He didn't think student leaders were paying attention to things that mattered, namely integration. He wanted to make sure students, particularly with the black-white ratio now more equal, were working together. He decided to run for student body president. He was a long shot and he knew it, unknown and inactive in student groups. Still, he put his name in at the office.

Being unknown and inactive had more problems than student recognition. The new principal, Bobby Matthews, told McRackan he wasn't qualified to run because he'd not participated in student government or other activities. Undeterred, McRackan consulted the student council constitution. Finding no language about those requirements, he took the document to Matthews and asked him to show him where it said he couldn't run. Matthews came back with another reason McRackan couldn't run: his hair was too long.

Frustrated, McRackan called Dufford. The next thing McRackan knew, Laughlin McDonald, head of the ACLU in South Carolina, arrived at Sumter High to speak to the principal. McDonald told Matthews that McRackan was within his rights to run and that a similar court case had already been won. It'd be bad publicity for Sumter High if McRackan weren't allowed his right to campaign. Matthews backed down, and McRackan benefited: "Word spread through the school like wildfire that they wouldn't let me run, because I didn't have a dog's chance in hell of winning."

McRackan's obscurity disappeared and he'd been given another reason to run—boys had the right to long hair.

With the green light to run for office, McRackan figured he'd talk to Dufford about his campaign speech. They decided to meet in person, at the Circus Room restaurant in lower Richland County. It was thirteen miles out of Sumter city limits—far enough to ensure privacy. Not long after, McRackan was confronted by Grady Locklear, head of the English department. He said he'd heard McRackan had been meeting with Dufford. McRackan was shocked. He would always wonder if he, in his "totally junk" '69 American Rambler, had been followed.

The Sheriff, the Klan, and Sandwiches Made by Good White Women

In September 1970, after Bill Dufford had left Sumter and as students at the newly named Sumter High School were adapting to full integration, a new splinter group of the KKK met outside town. The Invisible Empire, Knights of the Ku Klux Klan, realm of South Carolina, rallied at the Sumter Speedway. The group's founder, Robert E. Scoggin of Spartanburg, had led the 1961 effort to form the United Klans of America. Now he was three months into forming the IEKKKK and headlining the Sumter event. It quickly became obvious that serious trouble was brewing between the Klan's different factions.

Walter McRackan was there. Bored and looking for something to do, he stuffed his long hair under a ball cap, got a couple of his buddies, and went. What unfolded that Sunday, September 13, was something he never forgot: a man was shot and killed.

"It was like, 'Holy smoke, did you see that?' At that age, you're not smart enough to have proper fear," McRackan said. "It was like being in a wreck. You don't get the shakes until it's over."

From where he was standing, McRackan could see the impetus of the violence. Sumter resident Walter B. "Red" Brown, a UKA member, was on the front row, leaning forward to tape record speeches made by IEKKKK leaders. IEKKKK security guards tried to stop him, and heated words were exchanged. Brown said he'd erase the tape, but not give it up. When a guard realized Brown rewound the tape instead of erasing it, bedlam broke out.

"The Klan kept whistles under their robes, and one guy blew it," McRackan said. "That's a signal that 'we got trouble.' Pistols came out from every one of those robes."

Brown later testified he'd been beaten about the head with clubs while trying to leave, with IEKKKK members trying to take the tape recorder. Also trying to leave was Willie L. Odom, a fifty-year-old owner of a small Sumter grocery store and UKA member. Odom was shot in the back of the head and killed. McRackan recalled watching Odom's car hit a drainage ditch while trying to leave the raceway, and being unable to figure out if he hit the ditch because he was shot or if he hit the ditch and then was shot.

Future court testimony would reveal that Odom's wife and two sons were in the car with him, and that he decided to leave the rally after the altercation erupted over Brown's tape recorder. The boys were in the car when the shots were fired. His widow suffered two cracked ribs.

The incident resulted in ten Klansmen from various towns in South Carolina being charged with conspiracy to commit robbery—of the tape recorder—and accessory to murder. Scoggin was one of the ten. None of the men charged would say who actually killed Odom. Days later, IEKKKK "security chief" Carl Wildes of Andrews would be charged with malicious mischief and assault and battery of a high and aggravated nature. Joe Turner of Florence, a "security colonel," would be charged with murder. Except for Turner, who was kept at the Sumter County jail, all were released on bond. Eventually their charges were dropped.

Journalist Jack Bass, who'd covered the Orangeburg Massacre for the *Charlotte Observer* in 1968, reported on the Sumter slaying for the *Washington Post*. In his story, he wrote that I. Byrd Parnell said the murder was the first Klan trouble he'd experienced in his eighteen years as sheriff of Sumter County. Sam McCuen, covering the case for *The State* in Columbia, remembered how "livid" Parnell was that the Klan had come to his county.

Turner was arraigned in May 1971 and pleaded innocent to an indictment of murder. On November 9, 1971, he was acquitted in Sumter County General Sessions Court. The jury was all-white. The three teenage boys who'd heard someone of Turner's description say "I got him" after shots were fired declined to identify anyone in the courtroom that day, the *Sumter Item* reported.

After the shooting, Scoggin would be quoted in newspapers saying school integration was why Klan membership was growing. Decades later, Walter McRackan would marvel about two things. The first was that after Scoggin's death in 2003, his green satin Klan robe and white hood would be donated to the Levine Museum of the New South in Charlotte. But the second, and most disturbing, was what Scoggin told the crowd at the beginning of that rally in 1970: "We've got sandwiches for sale made by good white women. No nigger hands have touched these sandwiches."

Chapter 39

⟡

Summer Study 1971

IN THE SUMMER OF 1971, a group of rising high school seniors in South Carolina, all incoming leaders of their student councils, gathered to work on integration matters. Specially chosen for their beliefs in racial equality, their mission was "to study and share information on student involvement with the secondary educational community of South Carolina," according to the report they published later that summer. The students, black and white, came from all across the state, and they would travel to different parts of South Carolina, interviewing students, dropouts, teachers, and administrators. They'd earn $300 for their eight weeks of work. Directing the study—funded by private foundations—was the Reverend Paul Beazley, a Presbyterian minister and USC guidance and counseling graduate student. Their immediate supervisor was David Abel, a Robert Kennedy Fellow and Harvard doctoral student in education administration. Bill Dufford was one of twelve members on the advisory committee, a veritable who's who of South Carolina education leaders.

Two of the students—white boys with long hair—became fast friends: Richard Gergel, incoming president of Columbia's new Keenan High, and Walter McRackan, who'd won the race in Sumter. Both younger than eighteen, they were practically veterans of the integration fight. At the behest of Richland District 1 superintendent Claud Kitchens, also on the advisory committee, Gergel would run for school board the following year to refute the anti-integration message of Deadline '72. He didn't win, and didn't expect to, but he was able to argue from an insider's perspective that integration wasn't to be feared. Black voters turned out in droves to support him. Another "student director," Barbara Flemming of Eastover, also ran for the District 1 Board in 1972. She'd been vice president of the student council at Lower Richland High and, as a young black woman, was quoted as saying she was representing those three minorities—African Americans, women, and youth.

The students met at the CIE in Columbia, and at the historic Penn Center in Beaufort, where Abel advised them. McRackan remembers working "morning, noon, and night" on the program and a question-naire for the people they'd interview. They had a POGMA (Purpose, Objective, Goal, Mission, and Activity) chart. After a week of work, they were to present their research tools to the advisory board and have a photograph made for a brochure.

But there was one difficulty. McRackan's hair was too long. Abel advised he cut it. The students were already doing something controversial by participating in the study; they didn't need to overdo it. McRackan, who had run his campaign partly on students' rights to wear their hair however they wanted, balked. It'd be hypocritical to cut his hair.

A compromise was made. McRackan would wear a "short-hair wig" for the photograph and presentation. Dufford escorted McRackan to his barbershop in downtown Columbia, where he asked for a hairpiece that would work.

"It looked like hell," McRackan said years later, "like a bad Liberace haircut."

∽

Despite any difficulties with appearance, the students conducting the South Carolina Summer Study on Student Involvement got their work done. Like CIE staffers, they traveled in pairs. Collectively, they interviewed more than six hundred people in thirty-two high schools. Their findings were published in a report, the cover of which included snippets of what they learned.

"We learned partly how public education was failing kids, at-risk kids especially, and how there wasn't any magic to try to bring these kids back in, but it would take a real effort to do it," McRackan remembered. "You had to somehow make school interesting for kids. Kids were just bored out of their minds."

The kids chosen to conduct the study may or may not have been bored, but they were definitely interested in fairness, the future, and the important times in which they were living. Several went on to impressive careers: Barbara Flemming Weston became a legendary educator in Columbia and Orangeburg, winning the Milken Foundation Education Award in 1995. Michael Stephens of Dillon—participating when Ben Bernanke declined—became his district's public defender. Richard Gergel, who would maintain a lifelong friendship with Dufford, became a federal judge.

"It was really a fascinating period, a historic moment, and what was so interesting was that we knew it," Gergel said. "We knew we were in the middle of something really remarkable—the desegregation of the South—and we were on the front lines. I guess when you have a situation like that, you either run from it or you embrace it, and a lot of students wanted to embrace it. We had the moral fervor that we were involved in a great cause, and we had some converting of other people to do. That seemed inspiring."

Gergel's words would underscore Dufford's long-held beliefs about young people. "If you set the tone at the top that we're going to bring people together, kids are very flexible," Dufford would insist. "Adults are rigid. If you say, 'You gotta lead,' kids are very receptive."

"They did not want black boys dancing with white girls"

Perhaps one of the greatest casualties of early public school integration in South Carolina was the prom. Many high schools eliminated it. Judge Richard Gergel, student council president at Columbia's Keenan High in 1971–1972, remembers those days well.

"Let me tell you what they were really worried about: it wasn't just the violence at night. They didn't want interracial couples to come to the prom."

An outspoken advocate for integration, Gergel said interracial couples "absolutely" existed in his high school days. A good friend of his, an African American, was afraid about his relationship with a white girl he later married. "Nature occurs. You put people together, they date. Among my friends they were completely accepted."

Adults, though, often felt differently. "They did not want black boys dancing with white girls at those proms. They didn't know if they could handle that. Would white boys then attack the black kids? You know, who knows? All this stuff is about sex—race and sex—when you really get down to the bottom of it. All that racial separation—why do we have to be separated? It was to keep these lurking, lurching black men away from these white damsels. It was ridiculous. I think it's at the whole bottom of Jim Crow."

Fear drove other decisions. Basketball games, normally played at night, were rescheduled for afternoons. "To many black students this is saying, 'We don't trust you niggers,'" Gergel wrote in the winter 1971 issue of *New South: A Quarterly Review of Southern Affairs*. He also noted that in trying to bring black and white students together, one white church in Columbia lost half its congregation because the meeting was held there.

"I'm telling you, there was a lot of tension. All these ministers were racial progressives and their congregations were not. How do we accommodate this new reality out there?"

Coming from a Jewish family, Gergel knew what it was like to be on the fringes of southern society. His parents and other Columbia Jews—while not marching for civil rights—were quietly supportive of integration. "The people who didn't like African Americans didn't particularly like Jews either," he said. "Jews had this feeling of being 'the other,' but they didn't want to have the wrath of the angry white mob on them."

Still, the Columbia Jewish Community Center agreed to accommodate one hundred Keenan students—fifty white and fifty black, plus their parents—when Bill Dufford and Moses Rabb at the Center for Integrated Education presented a day-long program during Gergel's senior year. And Gergel's parents, Meri and Mel, never stopped their son from his political activities or entertained ideas of sending him and his brother, Randy, to private schools.

"My parents were chameleons. They blended in. They weren't looking for a fight. They weren't public about anything they did, but they quietly taught their children about decency and the way you treat people, the Golden Rule."

As it turned out, Keenan—a brand-new school at the time, with no culture or history—did relatively okay with integration. Its 50–50 black-white student population—mostly middle class, from the black Greenview and white Forest Acres neighborhoods—broke down more along economic lines, Gergel recalled. The middle-class students, well-dressed and college-bound, seemed worlds away from the less fortunate black and white students whose neighborhoods also were zoned for Keenan.

"There was definitely a class thing," he recalled. "The poor white kids and the poor black kids did not get along, and there was a lot of jawing and pushing and shoving, and a few incidents of actual violence. It was like the last rearguard opposition to school integration."

Chapter 40

༜

Boston Calling

D AVID ABEL'S Boston, Massachusetts, connections prompted an invitation from that city in 1972. Mayor Kevin White asked if the CIE could help their schools with integration. South Boston, largely white, would be integrating with mostly black Roxbury within two years. The black-white adult team of Moses Rabb and Bill Dufford would go with the black-white student team of Barbara Flemming and Walter McRackan. Flemming had just graduated from Lower Richland High; McRackan from Sumter.

Rabb and Dufford planned sessions in which the South Carolina students would meet with Boston students. Boston-area teachers also would participate. All parties assembled for a week on Cape Cod, and Rabb, the small group expert, prepared to lead the sessions. The first session began at night. But the next day, a group of Boston teachers boycotted.

"They said there would be no meeting," Rabb recalled. "They said we're not having outsiders coming in telling them what they're going to do."

Mayor White sent an assistant who announced that the teachers "would either have to cooperate as you've been directed or pack up and leave," Rabb said. "And he gave them 15 minutes to make that decision."

It wasn't a successful trip, and Dufford doubted, with only four South Carolinians to facilitate meetings, that it could be. Still, they tried, conducting sessions each day. Not surprisingly, the students on both sides got along well. At night, though, the white adults would "brainwash" them, Dufford would say.

"We'd walk by their cabins at night, and we'd hear the counselors talking to the Boston students and telling them not to listen. They convinced them this wasn't a good thing to do."

Years later, Rabb reflected that the South Carolina team, despite its success record and experience, was not equipped to deal with unions. "The unnecessary tension brought about by that kind of thing was different. We had some good kids, hard-working kids, but obviously some of them had to do what their parents told them to do. Their parents were beholden to some of the union people and other folk who didn't want to see it work." It also probably wasn't easy for educators in the North to listen to educators from the South, Rabb said.

The foursome returned to South Carolina frustrated. Boston's Mayor White sent a thank-you note. When desegregation started in Boston in 1974, Irish whites from the south Boston area—called "Southies"—threw rocks and bricks at buses carrying black children to school from Roxbury—a predominately black section of midtown Boston.

"He broke down every stereotype"

David Abel was twenty-five, with long hair, a beard, and a Robert Kennedy Fellowship, when he was "parachuted" into South Carolina in 1970. His fellowship focused on working with newly elected and appointed African American school board members. Stationed in Hayes Mizell's office on the corner of Main and Gervais Streets in Columbia, Abel soon met Bill Dufford at USC's Center for Integrated Education. For Abel, whose roots were in California and the Northeast, observing Dufford at work was unforgettable.

"Watching Bill engage and listen to conversations and set an example through his own work—he broke down every stereotype someone outside the South would have," Abel said, recalling country-fried steak suppers they attended in towns across the state. "I learned how to deal with people I was going to confront in an open way, and understand the challenges of high school students, which I thought I knew and didn't."

As a former Coro Foundation Fellow, Abel earlier had recognized the importance of working with young people, future leaders who'd be living in a more integrated world. The CIE's Summer Study program was modeled after a similar CORO program, "hatched" in Mizell's office. Once the students had been selected, Abel took charge that summer of 1971. The experience was "incredible," with Abel realizing he'd found valued mentors in Mizell and Dufford. He'd also watched Dufford and Moses Rabb working together. "The two of them? Unbelievable."

Back in law school at Boston University the next year, Abel thought the Summer Study program might work there. Integrating schools in African American Roxbury and white Irish South Boston—or Southie—was of particular concern. He pitched his idea to Rob Hamilton, executive director of Joe Hill Associates, named after the famed labor leader executed in 1915. "I said, 'I'd love to take these people away from South Boston and I've got just the right mentors, the consultants. I can raise the money.'"

Hamilton agreed, and with money from the City of Boston and private foundation money from the Friends of the Kennedy Memorial, the foursome of Dufford, Rabb, McRackan, and Flemming were invited to Cape Cod in June

1972, where they stayed in the same cabins in which Dufford's navy radar team had stayed during training in 1945.

The outcome of the foursome's efforts was not what Abel envisioned.

"The racism was fiercer in Boston," Abel recalled. Southie was a very insular, Irish place, and tough for anybody to penetrate, especially an African American. The idea that they would change the culture in Southie was fiercely opposed. When we brought the students together, I found the Southie kids much tougher, more ready to fight physically than I imagined. It was disappointing."

The South Carolina students had been the opposite, Abel said. "They were like most South Carolinians—good people. They weren't looking for a fight. They were looking for a way to work together. That wasn't the case in Boston."

Eventually Abel and his group awarded a handful of grants to start new programs in the South Boston-Roxbury school system. "But the feeling, the flavor, the culture of that retreat was not as generous and warm and open and constructive as the Summer Study, which was a particularly popular experience."

Now in Los Angeles, David Abel stays in touch with those with whom he worked in South Carolina. "If you're ever going to go into a new situation that's going to test your human spirit and idealism, go into it with a mentor like Bill Dufford. He and Hayes were living, breathing subjects. Bill was this incredible force of 'This can be done. I know the people who want to do it, I know we can do it.' You never dwelled on the negative—'it's impossible.' It's 'Sure, we can do it, and let's have fun while we do.' I'm still a fan of South Carolina because of Bill Dufford."

Chapter 41

༄

The Deepening, Widening Circle

DUFFORD'S BRASH FRIENDLINESS and talent for mentoring high school boys made him something of a human tornado, picking up friends everywhere he went. By the mid-1970s he'd collected a number of former students who gravitated to his place in Columbia on Saturday afternoons. They'd play basketball and talk, and young men who didn't know each other before became acquainted and often friends thereafter.

Richard Gergel and Walter McRackan were regulars; Allen Johnson, by now married and playing baseball at USC, came by when he could. Pat Conroy would show up; back in Sumter he'd met Reed Swann, whose young daughters he babysat.

At first the gang met at Dufford's St. Andrews-area apartment. He rented a room to a former Beaufort student, Jeff Greene, who cooked their meals in exchange for rent. In 1970 Dufford took some advice from Billy Jones, a former student from Beaufort. Jones suggested he invest in real estate: there were properties in downtown Columbia and West Columbia he could buy. Prices were particularly reasonable because families were leaving the city for majority white schools in the suburbs.

Dufford's purchase of a rambling brick home in the Hollywood-Rose Hill neighborhood, a duplex apartment on Princess Street, and another dwelling across the river in Cayce meant he could make money as a landlord. He had a built-in clientele—his former students and their friends attending USC. Tim Conroy, the second-youngest in the Conroy family, became a tenant and devoted friend. McRackan also rented from Dufford in the later 1970s.

It had to have been gratifying to watch his students grow and take up his philosophy about integration. Walter McRackan may have been the greatest example. As president of Sumter High in 1971–1972, he was on fire. He'd forged a strong bond with Shirley Chatman, a black girl who'd been elected vice president, and the duo worked to bring their races together. McRackan learned to get advice from sympathetic Vice Principal Ethel Burnett about making changes, and on some matters he and Chatman sidestepped the principal and superintendent and went straight to the board. There was an African American board member now, Jim Solomon, and he and another white member, Dr. Charles Propst, were receptive to McRackan and Chatman. The board gave them permission to reinstate the prom and school dances after football games.

Throughout the year, McRackan would consult Dufford. Knowing he wouldn't be welcomed by Sumter's upper administration, Dufford suggested McRackan and Chatman solicit help from his colleagues at the CIE. Moses Rabb and Burnett Joiner, another CIE staffer, would teach Sumter High students to become small group facilitators, leading black and white students in homeroom "rap sessions." The sessions were designed to help break barriers between the races so they could be educated together in harmony. They worked well enough for the National Education Association to cover them in its *Today's Education* magazine. "Rapping in Sumter High" appeared in the February 1971 issue.

"The biggest thing that changed was the relationships that developed between kids," McRackan recalled of the rap sessions. "A lot of misunderstandings would be cleared up. Kids got comfortable enough where they were laughing and giggling and cutting the fool. The white kids asked black kids about their hair, like, 'Do you do anything to your hair to make it look like that?' And black kids would say, 'Since you bring it up, what do you do to *your* hair?' It wasn't that earthshaking; it was more of people being able to relax and get along with each other a little bit as equals—which was huge, if you think about what was going on. Because we always had relationships with each other, blacks and whites, but there'd been no parity to it."

McRackan's success came with a price. His beliefs caused some of his friends to sever ties with him, including those who veered off into private schools. But as had Dufford, he was moving into a more diverse world, one that was changing dramatically. Sumter wasn't immune. The white boys' clubs that had been so popular—the Les Rois and Esquires—disappeared, just as tailored clothing dissolved into bell-bottomed jeans and tie-dyed shirts.

Besides, McRackan made new friends. Black and white, they hung out together, sometimes in fast food joints, sometimes in the home of State Representative Ernest A. Finney Jr. and his wife, Frances. Their son, Chip, was a junior that year. McRackan knew some black and white kids were making friends through athletics, he and others through "mutual contempt for the administration of the high school." Either way, he was experiencing what Dufford already knew, that kids could reach out to others when adults could not. And that was with or without rap sessions.

"There were black kids with a yearning for success equal or greater than that of white kids," McRackan recalled. "You didn't have to break your neck to make the effort. There were lots of olive branches being put out by kids. If you made a little bit of effort, the response was huge."

Two years after his departure, Bill Dufford's influence was still at work in Sumter.

"If that ain't living the faith, nothing is"

No doubt it took plenty of chutzpah to run for school board as a seventeen-year-old, but Richard Gergel was up for the challenge. He believed integration was the right thing to do, he believed schools would be better served if students had a stronger voice, and he knew, during that momentous year of 1972, that he had a mighty support system of mentors. Besides Bill Dufford, there were Hayes Mizell, David Abel, Paul Beazley, and Isadore Lourie, the noted Columbia lawmaker who, perhaps because of his Jewishness, was able to help black and white people in the 1960s connect.

Gergel also had friends who believed as he did, many of whom he met through Dufford. He was a regular at Dufford's place on Saturdays for basketball—Dufford and Pat Conroy were particularly aggressive, he recalled—but there was more connecting them than sports.

"It was kindred spirits. Most seventeen–eighteen year-olds aren't particularly interested in politics, race, current affairs. They're usually partying, drinking, and having a big time. Those of us who had those interests hung out with each other, and it ended up being a pretty interesting predictor of future success in life, because this crowd has been pretty remarkably successful."

Gergel and others who rotated around Dufford became friends with those who wrote for the upstart *Osceola* newspaper, an activist publication covering South Carolina politics and social issues in the 1970s. Staffers included Richard Harpootlian, a much-quoted Columbia lawyer who became chairman of the state Democratic party, and Tim Rogers, another Columbia lawyer and ten-year member of the state legislature.

"You know how the Chinese say 'let me be reborn in important times'? These were important times, and we were right on the front line. We thought we were on a wave of seeing the future."

But they miscalculated the future, Gergel said. Integration hasn't worked as well as they hoped. White flight changed districts, and middle-class African Americans don't live in poor districts with low-achieving schools. Resegregation has occurred.

"It was the end of an era, more than what we thought would be the beginning of one. But you never give up hope, right? And we keep finding our best path to have influence for good."

A federal judge who has written extensively about civil rights, Gergel has Bill Dufford for a role model. Dufford's return to the classroom after his work in Sumter and York will forever be something he admires. "Here he was, he could have gone back to any college and taught, and he went back and taught math to poor kids at Eau Claire High School. I mean, if that ain't living the faith, nothing is."

Chapter 42

༄

From the Frying Pan to the Fire

DUFFORD ENJOYED HIS WORK and colleagues at the Center for Integrated Education. He was doing some different things— teaching a USC graduate course on high school principalship, running a closed-circuit TV program that allowed lectures and interactions to be shared with school board members across the state about best practices. Besides Moses Rabb, the CIE's director of school-community relations, he met two other men who played important roles in his life. One was Dr. J. C. Holler, who worked at the CIE through his job at the state Department of Education. The other was Burnett Joiner, an education doctoral student from Mississippi. Holler, a white man from York County, was nearing the end of his career. Joiner, who was black, was just beginning—though he already recognized he could earn more money as a graduate student in South Carolina than as a principal with a master's degree in Mississippi.

In some ways, Dufford felt like his work at the CIE was akin to that of first responders. "We were called in like firemen," he recalled. "The fire had started before we got there."

So, in 1974, when Holler suggested Dufford take the superintendent's job at York County District 1, he listened. It was another opportunity coming to him, not one he sought. Dufford had a lot of respect for Holler.

"He put my name in the pot and he says, 'You need to go. Those people need help.' I just trusted people, particularly people I liked."

It was no secret that elsewhere in York County serious problems had erupted. On January 26, 1972, more than two hundred black students walked out of the integrated Rock Hill High when the band director forced students to play "Dixie." The students marched to their former school, Emmett Scott Senior High, singing their alma mater. Finding their old school closed, they asked Rock Hill High's principal, Calvin Burleson, for a meeting the next day. They were directed to the auditorium, where they learned state and city law enforcement had been called. A riot had been predicted, and officers with riot control gear arrived. Burleson dismissed school at 10:30 that morning and, under pressure from York District 3 superintendent Jeff Savage, refused to talk to the students. The students were suspended for three days.

York County's integration problems weren't restricted to Rock Hill High. At Fort Mill High, black students from the former George Fish Elementary and the black high schools waged a sit-in to protest the loss of their school colors. They asked for more black teachers, the addition of black cheerleaders, coaches, principals, and trustees, a more equal discipline code, and athletic opportunities for girls. They also wanted the George Fish alma mater incorporated with the Fort Mill alma mater. The February 29, 1972, sit-in ended with police officers escorting the students to jail. Tear gas was used.

The difficulties at Rock Hill High came to a head on March 2, 1972. That day 180 black students marched from Rock Hill High to Superintendent Savage's office. Many broke the windows of businesses and street lights on the way. The school board didn't meet any of the students' demands, and Savage suspended all 180 of them for three days.

York District 1 wasn't experiencing that kind of violence. The district encompassed the quaint, historic county seat of York and the area immediately around it. Three high schools were in the district—the majority-white York High, the black Jefferson High, and the rural, mostly white Hickory Grove. Desegregation effort had already begun, and Jefferson was operating as a junior high. Hickory Grove students would come in when a new high school was built.

Guided not just by his respect for Holler, Dufford knew there was another good reason to take the job: Reed Swann was principal of York High. They'd worked well together before, why not again? Dufford accepted the job and named Swann assistant superintendent. He asked Burnett Joiner to come too. Swann would direct operations and finance; Joiner would handle curriculum, instruction, and personnel. With two trusted friends in place, Dufford prepared to move.

Steve Satterfield, coaching at Wofford College at the time, guffawed when he heard Dufford was going to York. "He better start running backwards so the community can keep up," he said.

Chapter 43

༺

Welcome to York

W HAT FACED DUFFORD in York District 1 was classic desegregation, not integration. Black and white students were being educated on one campus, but there was little unity between them. Except for black students, who came in the fall of 1970 when Jefferson High closed, nearly everything about York High—home of the Green Dragons—remained the same. The black students had been told their concerns about the school name, colors, and mascot would be addressed as soon as the new school was built and the Hickory Grove students joined them.

"During the process of integration, there were only three things that were important to communities, and they had nothing to do with curriculum or teacher preparation or proposed leadership," Dufford said. "They cared about the name of the school, the colors, and the mascot. It had nothing to do with the process of educating kids, but that's the way people identify with their school."

To let the populace know a black man would be working in a high position at the district office, Dufford invited Joiner to walk around downtown York with him. The men strolled in their coats and ties, with Dufford introducing himself as the new superintendent and Joiner as assistant superintendent. The visits were cordial, until they stopped in at a drugstore. The pharmacist, a recent school board member, casually mentioned he didn't know a new black assistant superintendent had replaced the one who had just retired. That gentleman had been a principal at Jefferson High. When the schools were desegregated, he'd been brought to the district office—essentially a demotion for an educator who works with students, but a way to "placate the black citizens" by allowing him to keep some form of employment with a title, Dufford said.

Disappointed by the druggist's reaction, Dufford nevertheless responded that Joiner had indeed been hired. And he persisted in not only keeping Joiner public—at school board meetings and other education gatherings—but in giving him opportunities to prove himself and empowering him to make decisions. Many black educators who'd been shunted off to district offices after desegregation had been placed in positions of low responsibility.

"If you wanted to work, you had no other recourse than to accept whatever opportunity was made available to you," Joiner said. "The principals didn't want to abandon the black students or the black community. Consequently, they went with whatever was offered."

In his late twenties and already hardened to the realities of segregation, Joiner didn't recognize the druggist's comment for the disguised put-down it was. Dufford had to point it out from his past experiences. "He was sensitive to a lot of that," Joiner said. "He knew what stuff meant that I wouldn't be able to read."

Not long after, Dufford and Joiner drove to Rock Hill for a regular meeting of York County's four district superintendents and other upper administrators. Only white men made up the group.

"It was like a deer looking at headlights," Dufford said. "It was, 'What in the hell is he doing here?'"

This time Joiner knew he'd been a surprise. "They looked around, kind of shocked. It was like, 'I've seen a ghost.' Of course, they quickly got composure because Dufford acted like I was supposed to be there."

Joiner and Dufford knew the white superintendents had black subordinates on their staffs, but they weren't decision makers who would be included in such a meeting. Joiner was the first.

Chapter 44

⟳

A New Team

I T HAD BEEN FOUR YEARS since Bill Dufford and Reed Swann had worked together in Sumter, and they looked forward to working together again in York. Swann knew Dufford's views on integration differed from those of Harold Johnson, the superintendent who had just retired. In 1970, fresh off his year in Sumter, Swann had entered Johnson's office with a copy of the *State* newspaper, excited about the story that York 1's plans to integrate had been approved by the U.S. Department of Education's Office for Civil Rights. York would be the first district in South Carolina to integrate. Johnson, Swann learned quickly, didn't share his excitement. "He was about to have a stroke that we were going to lead the way," Swann recalled.

Still, Jefferson and York High Schools merged according to law, and Swann, who'd been hired as Johnson's administrator, had been sent to be principal at York High when the previous principal died. There, he'd dealt with black students who were upset that their mascot, colors, and school name had not been adopted or incorporated into their new school. Swann duly reported their concerns to Johnson, who said those concerns would be "considered." When the new high school was built and Hickory Grove included, all those matters would be decided, Swann was told.

He knew Dufford, as superintendent, would make sure black students were heard and their needs addressed.

While plans for the new school were being made, Swann, Dufford, and Burnett Joiner settled down to the business of educating the students of York 1. Dufford, Joiner would say, was "the visionary," the one who would notice they had students who were hungry and others who were sick. Many parents were migrant or mill workers, up and out of the house before the sun. Dufford decided their schools needed to serve breakfast.

"It was a concern," Dufford said. "I inquired why we weren't serving these kids breakfast and a school secretary/bookkeeper, who was white, said that the lunchroom workers, who were black, didn't want to do it. So I said, 'Let me speak to all the lunchroom workers.' They all assembled. The first thing that we found out is that they were anxious to do it because it meant more money. This is one instance again of where school districts or corporate America didn't want to provide services. Well, we started serving breakfast the next week."

Several schools in the state also had nurses; Dufford decided York needed one too. Joiner, handling personnel, found two exceptional nurses who more than suited their needs. Only able to pay one, Dufford suggested hiring both and making one a social worker, a critical professional for a rural, underserved community. An attendance officer and school psychologist were hired. Joiner also worked on grants for other programs, and through more of his efforts York High started its first Advanced Placement courses, in chemistry, English, and math. Quiet, reserved, and working long hours, Joiner became a beloved administrator by the teachers.

The Dufford-Swann-Joiner trio was a winning team. The men were friends in and out of the district office, sometimes having lunch in town or in school cafeterias. Joiner would call Dufford a "Pied Piper," someone whose extroverted personality drew people of all ages to him and made them comfortable. But he was also a canny businessman, aware of how school district purchases would be viewed. When new school vehicles needed to be bought, Swann followed district policy and planned to buy from companies that bid the lowest, Joiner recalled. Dufford looked at it another way: a few hundred dollars wasn't a big difference if you could buy from a dealer in the district. "What kind of message is that to send the local dealership for their support over the long run that we would garner from them?" Dufford had pointed out.

Dufford, Joiner said, could zero in on the small things while always keeping the main objective at the forefront. "Reed and I would get caught up in stuff and processes, and he would bring us back to 'Is this in the best interest of kids?' I thought we were very effective in the work we did."

Chapter 45

❧

Impossible to Say No

TRUTH BE TOLD, Burnett Joiner had no real desire to go to York. He was happy in Columbia, where he was working on his dissertation at USC and completing his education specialist degree. He had already come so far, much further than his family in Raymond, Mississippi, ever would have thought. His going to college, much less earning his master's degree and doctorate, was beyond their imaginations.

There had been no dreams of being an astronaut or president for young Burnett Joiner. Teacher and principal were the most astonishing careers he could envision. And he'd pursued them, earning a bachelor's degree at historically black Alcorn State University near Lorman, Mississippi, and a master's from Bradley University in Peoria, Illinois. Black students in segregated Mississippi couldn't attend state schools for degrees higher than a bachelor's, though state funds were provided to pay for their graduate school out of state. So that's what Joiner did, leaving Mississippi on a bus from Jackson in 1964. In Peoria, he'd have his first white professor and be one of very few black students in his class—a lonely, frightening experience for someone already introverted and far from home. Sick with anxiety, he didn't attend class for a week, and planned to quit. Then his friendly, white, female professor intercepted him, chatted him up, said, "You're going places, I can tell," and Joiner unpacked his bags. He eventually made friends, got his master's, and returned to Mississippi to help those he left behind, accompanied by a classmate he married. He was a principal in Clarksdale and a father of one when he was recruited to work at the Center for Integrated Education at USC. That's where he met Bill Dufford.

Joiner knew Dufford had undergone a radical change in his thinking about race. Joiner never knew *that* Bill Dufford. "By the time I met him, if he was prejudiced, I couldn't tell it," he would say. "I thought he was one of the fairest people I have ever met, black or white."

He was also one of the most outgoing. Joiner would observe him, talking, hugging, putting his hand on the shoulder of the student or teacher he was advising. Joiner, whose mother had told him never to look at or speak to a white woman, found himself adopting Dufford's friendly manner. At teacher trainings the CIE presented, Joiner would instruct white teachers about teaching black children and black teachers about teaching white children. It was only natural in group or class discussions for his hand to rest on the back of a desk or chair, and sometimes on a teacher's shoulder.

Then one day the CIE got a notice. A teacher in Winnsboro—white and female—had filed a complaint that Burnett Joiner had touched her shoulder. The CIE, with its staff of black and white educators, told him about the call and shrugged it off. But Burnett Joiner would never touch another teacher again—ever—in his distinguished career. He would, however, listen to whatever Bill Dufford had to say. And when Dufford asked him to take the job in York, he said yes, though he really would have preferred to stay where he was. Joiner was one of many who learned through the years that when Bill Dufford asked you to do something, it was just impossible to say no.

Chapter 46

❧

Learning the District

DUFFORD LIKED YORK. Scouting the area in his Volvo, he thought he might buy a house there. Burnett Joiner was living in Rock Hill, commuting fourteen miles to work. Reed Swann and his wife, Hunter, a teacher, had just built a house in the country. Assistant district superintendent was a top job in public education, and he'd achieved it.

One thing Dufford knew was that in rural areas the high school agriculture teacher had stature. In York District 1, that person was Floyd Johnson. He'd been teaching there for thirty-five years and knew the families, the farmers, and the members of the all-white, all-male school board. It didn't take long for Dufford to learn Johnson wasn't in favor of integration in terms of race or gender: He wouldn't let a girl enroll in his ag class.

During Dufford's first year in York, the high school went through the arduous process of accreditation by the Southern Association of Colleges and Schools. Cecil Tucker, with USC's College of Education, came to York High as chair of the SACS visitation committee. In the auditorium, on stage with Tucker and the high school's co-presidents—one black, one white—Dufford listened in shock to Tucker's presentation to the students.

"He complimented the school on their work toward integrating the student body," Dufford recalled. "I'm looking at the student body—blacks on one side and whites on the other side—and he's complimenting the student council members on what a great job they had done to bring integration to the school. I'm thinking, 'Jesus, there's no process of integration to the audience." Even professors at Carolina thought if blacks and whites were in the same room, they were integrated."

After Tucker's presentation, Dufford huddled with the two student council presidents to voice his embarrassment and concern. "We've got to do better than this," he told them. But later, the mother of the black student called Dufford, upset about the conversation her son reported. She was a teacher who felt her son had been "reprimanded" unfairly.

"You're protective of your own child and you don't want your child to be chastised, but there's a bigger issue about bringing people together,"

Dufford reasoned years later. "All these kids came from parents raised in the Jim Crow South and an awful lot of parents think all we have to do is let them in the door. But all kids need equal treatment. It's the same old thing of making blacks sit at the back of the bus. 'They're on the bus, so why aren't they happy?' Because being present is not the same thing as being treated equally."

Dufford would learn that elsewhere in South Carolina white teachers would make their black students sit in the back of the room. Luci Vaden, the USC doctoral history student, would report that some white teachers in the state turned their backs on black students while teaching.

It irked Dufford for years that at Rock Hill High the only concession made to the new black students was a gold stripe down their football uniform pants.

Chapter 47

❧

Decision at Hickory Knob

IN 1975, during his second school year in York, Dufford knew action would have to be taken on choosing a school name, mascot, and colors. Thinking students in York, like those in Sumter, could make those decisions, he asked the student council president at York High if he'd be willing to start discussions with other students. Interested at first, the student soon declined. Dufford said he later learned Floyd Johnson, the powerful agriculture teacher, had dissuaded the student through his parents. "We wanted students to work on such issues, but adults had gotten hold of them. Parents had learned what we'd done in Sumter and they didn't want to do that."

Dufford, Swann, and Joiner conferred. Their Plan B was faculty. Could respected members from each of the district's nine schools make the decision? They asked the principals of each to choose one teacher who'd earned a good reputation at school and in the community. Together, this committee could hammer out a fair compromise, the men thought. The principals agreed, teachers were chosen, and Moses

Rabb, the small group expert at the CIE, was solicited to facilitate their discussions with the help of a white colleague. The group, black and white, would spend time during a week at Hickory Knob State Park in McCormick County to make a decision. Dufford knew it was important for them to meet out of town.

"They couldn't stay in their community and be dealing with this; they would have people knocking on the door. This was intense stuff. You better believe everybody who finished York High School wanted to be the green and white Green Dragons, in the same manner that everybody at Jefferson wanted to be the blue and white Blue Devils, and everybody at Hickory Grove wanted it to be the red and white Cardinals. If we don't understand the intensity of the way people feel about their school and identify with their colors and their mascots, we are living in a world with blinders."

The committee gathered before they left. Dufford, Swann, Joiner, Rabb, his CIE colleague, and the school principals attended the meeting. Dufford spoke. He asked specifically for a decision on colors, mascot, and name of the school. He reinforced the message he'd been preaching since his days at the University of Florida: "We don't want to leave anybody out. We want everyone to feel a part of the new school."

The teachers listened, and one had a question: "If we come back with a recommendation, are y'all going to support us?"

Dufford said he would, signaling his respect for teachers and principals. Then the principal at York High countered, saying he couldn't promise any support until he heard what decision had been made. Dufford took note of the comment, and the group departed.

Once situated at Hickory Knob, the CIE team got to work. They knew they had several dynamics to monitor. Not only could there be mistrust between the white teachers at York and the black teachers at Jefferson, there could be friction between the small-town white teachers in York and the rural white teachers at Hickory Grove. Hickory Grove did have a few African American students, the children of the school's custodians and cooks, but the white social structure dominated the whole district. It was the CIE team's duty to get the teachers to relax and talk about unimportant things, find common ground in those unimportant things, and then move discussions to the decisions that had to be made. "I had to be alert to their feelings and needs," Rabb recalled. "I was responsible for people not getting hurt."

Sequestered for five days during the week—the district considered their mission important enough to pay them for it—the teachers slowly became comfortable with each other. They ate together in the park's dining hall, choosing not to partake in any of its outdoor recreational offerings. Not as quickly, but just as surely as the students at Edmunds and Lincoln High Schools in Sumter came together to make their decision, the York District 1 teachers made theirs. "It was a feeling of relief," Rabb said. "It was a feeling of 'look what they did,' and it renews your faith in people."

For the CIE it was another victory, and confirmation of what they knew already. "Once we can get people attuned to how they're alike and drop their facades, positive movement begins to happen." The CIE team headed back to Columbia, and the teachers returned to York County.

A few days later the teacher committee gathered again. They had made a decision, and it was unanimous, as Dufford requested. Their choice for the new school's name was logical: York Comprehensive High School. Their choice for colors and mascot would be brand new, with no vestiges of York, Jefferson, or Hickory Grove. They chose black and silver for the school colors and cougars for the mascot. They presented their decision to Dufford, who presented it to the members of the school board at their next meeting.

Their reaction was measured. "They tepidly said, 'We'll take this, but let's study it,'" Dufford recalled.

The next day, Dufford dispatched Joiner to Jefferson Junior High and Swann to Hickory Grove to relay the choice the teacher group had made. He communicated the teachers' decision to the students and faculty at York High. Now it was a matter of waiting for the school board to approve or disapprove.

Chapter 48

ᶜᵛ

Tension Rising

THE DAY AFTER THE BOARD MEETING in which the proposed new colors, mascot, and school name were presented, Dufford got called to York High School. White students were throwing rocks at black students in the parking lot. Police were on their way. Dufford, in the administration building three blocks away, hurried over. He saw Floyd Johnson and a guidance counselor watching the ruckus from a window. Dufford, who attended plenty of ball games and other after-school activities, recognized the white students as Johnson's ag students.

"Floyd, those kids are all Ag Club kids," he said.

"Doc, I believe you're right," Johnson responded.

"You better go take care of them," Dufford instructed. Johnson, known for his slow walk and slow talk, moved toward the scene. The drama was over by the time he got there.

Dufford wasn't close enough to see how the black students reacted. He did know rock-throwing wouldn't lead to unity. And he fretted about York administrators breaking their word to the black community from Jefferson, those who asked for their voices to be heard when they were moved to York High. "They'd been *promised*," he would repeat decades later. A promise to a student, Dufford believed, was sacred.

As the school year progressed, the board made no decision on the committee's choices. Dufford started thinking they really weren't interested in fair integration. Meanwhile, notices began to appear around town. One advertised a "Public Meeting" at the York National Guard Armory.

ALL CITIZENS INTERESTED IN SHOWING THEIR SUPPORT FOR THE DULY ELECTED MEMBERS OF THE BOARD OF TRUSTEES OF YORK SCHOOL DISTRICT NUMBER I ARE INVITED TO ATTEND.

SUPPORT DUE PROCESS

ATTEND THE MEETING

The notice said the meeting was paid for by "Concerned Citizens & Students of York School District Number 1."

The meeting was scheduled for February 2. Also appearing around town were posters for a KKK Rally on March 1 behind the York Tractor Company. The event was described as "special," and included these words, warning of gang violence, which Dufford knew to be untrue:

Racial Beatings by Gangs Continue in York, SC.

DUE TO THE INFILTRATION OF THE N.A.A.C.P. AND OTHER BLACK COMMUNIST GROUPS, STUDENTS AND ALL WHITE PARENTS, TAX-PAYERS OF YORK S.C. HAVE ASKED THE KNIGHTS OF THE KU KLUX

KLAN FOR LEADERSHIP AND SUPPORT. WE RALLY AND WILL
SUPPORT WHITE PEOPLES RIGHTS UNTIL "HELL FREEZES OVER"
JOIN "TODAY" TO "LIVE TOMORROW"

SUPPORT THE WHITE MAN'S REVOLUTION!

In the space above "Featured Speaker" were these words: Grand Dragon
of SC., ASST DRAGON and students of York Hi along with parents
and taxpayers.

Dufford didn't attend the meeting or the rally. To him, the gatherings were planned to influence the board. But he knew the Klan's
power, and he knew Billy Martin, the popular and successful Jefferson
High coach, lost his job when the schools merged. Like many black
head coaches, Martin had been another casualty of integration, stripped
of even an assistant coaching position. He'd be teaching social studies
only, giving up the financial supplement that coaching provided and the
prestige in his community of being known as Coach Martin instead of
just Mr. Martin.

After the committee returned from Hickory Knob, Dufford got a
call from Martin before dawn. A cross was burning in his yard, perhaps
in response to Martin's complaint to the administration about his reas-
signment. In the dark, Dufford hurried to Martin's home to comfort
him and his family. "I had an obligation and responsibility to protect my
staff," Dufford recalled years later. "Back then, a burning cross meant
'we're going to lynch you next.'"

Having no friends at the police department and no expectation of
help from law enforcement, Dufford decided to let the situation die
down and to assure Martin that his safety was a priority. There were no
more incidents at the Martin home. Martin continued to teach in the
district, but he never coached again, Dufford said.

Burnett Joiner didn't learn about the happenings until later. He'd
been so focused, toiling late into the evenings, working on programs
for students.

Chapter 49

❧

Last Man Standing; or, Swann Song

A S SPRING WORE ON And no decision was made about the commit-tee's recommendations for the new school's colors, name, or mascot, Bill Dufford realized he and the decision makers in York District 1 were incompatible. He dictated a letter of resignation to Nancy McFarland, his secretary, and kept it beside him at school board meetings.

Meanwhile, evening meetings went on across the district for parents and other citizens to discuss the changes. Hearing rumors that violence might break out at a meeting at York High, Reed Swann got on the phone to South Carolina Attorney General Travis Medlock, his friend and classmate from Wofford. Medlock, who had also been a state senator and chief counsel for the South Carolina Education Association, put in a call to the State Law Enforcement Division. That evening, Medlock and an assistant attorney general walked into the meeting. "You could have heard a pin drop," Dufford remembered. No violence occurred.

Finally, the board made their decision. Chairman George Hart, a banker, made the announcement. A graduate of York High, Hart was the announcer at school football games. His words would stay with Dufford, Joiner, and Swann for years: "I'm the Voice of the Green Dragons, I was born a Green Dragon, and Lord willing, I will die a Green Dragon."

The board decided to keep all three schools' mascots and colors. The football team would remain the Green Dragons with green colors, the basketball team would be the Blue Devils with blue colors, and the baseball team would be the Cardinals with red colors. The school's name would be York Comprehensive High School.

For Dufford, it was a decision that not only disrespected him and the teacher committee but also proved the board and certain segments of the community didn't want or understand a unified school or true integration. The board agreed to buy out his contract.

Joiner and Swann, nearing the completion of two years of remark-able improvement in the district, knew their leader couldn't stay. The question was, could they?

It wasn't hard for Joiner to decide. He'd pulled out his dissertation that spring, polishing it up in his off-hours. He could tell the board wasn't enthusiastic about the committee's proposal, and as far as he was concerned, if Dufford left, he would too. He wrote a one-sentence letter stating he'd be leaving the district in the summer. Offers had arrived from Benedict, Winthrop, and South Carolina State. Educators were watching what was going on in York; he and his family wouldn't starve.

It wasn't so easy for Swann. He'd married into a York family. His wife, Hunter, taught in the district, their two daughters were in the schools. He'd worked for York District 1 for almost twenty years, rising to assistant superintendent, the highest you could go without a doctorate. And there was that new house he and Hunter had just built, out in the country. If anyone was invested and entrenched in York 1, it was Reed Swann.

But as it turned out, Swann knew what to do. And it was for him as much as it was for Bill Dufford, the teacher and coach who'd mentored him all those years ago, and who kept offering him jobs years later. At a subsequent board meeting—Dufford and Joiner now gone—Swann entered to find board members in a jovial mood. At the head of the table was Floyd Johnson, the ag teacher Dufford had learned had been meeting secretly with board members. Johnson had been named the new superintendent.

"They were talking and telling what a good year we're going to have under Floyd Johnson, and they asked me, 'What did I think?'" Swann recalled. "And I looked at Floyd Johnson and I said, 'I feel sorry for that man, because he doesn't know what he's getting into.' And I told them I was leaving, I was resigning."

It was a decision no one, save Hunter, knew was coming. Good old Reed Swann, quiet, dependable Reed Swann, had stood up and thrown it all away. After the shock, board members—at least one a former student—tried to get him to change his mind. Swann wouldn't be swayed.

"I said, 'I'll have a job. Don't worry. I'm not staying in this situation with that man.'" And he walked out of the room.

The next day he turned in a formal letter of resignation. Secretary Nancy McFarland handed him an audio tape. The recorder used to record the minutes had been turned on accidentally before the meeting started, and Swann's unexpected announcement and the ensuing conversation had been captured. He took the tape and went home to his new house in the country, and called Dufford and Joiner to come over.

"I've got something I want y'all to hear," he said.

He played the tape and watched his friends' amazement. Hunter, like many teachers in the district, appreciated what Dufford, Joiner, and Swann were doing. If her husband needed to leave, she and the children were going with him. For Swann, it was really just a matter of doing the right thing, no matter how hard it was.

"You have to look at yourself every morning when you shave," he said years later. "I really believed in what we were doing, and if these guys left and I stayed, how could I live with myself? Had I gone along with what was going on, what message would that send not only to me but my family, and me later on in life? How can you live with that feeling you'd been part of something that was right and this was wrong, and you went along with it?"

Those questions were just too easy to answer, and Reed, Hunter, Garnett, and Ouida Swann packed up and moved to Barnwell. Swann had landed the principal's job at Barnwell High. He'd be making the highest salary—$20,000—of any principal in South Carolina at the time.

"It's dead serious"

John Spratt was a lawyer in his early thirties when Bill Dufford came to York. Spratt, McKeown and Spratt represented—pro bono—York District 1, and Spratt or his partner Melvin McKeown were called for counsel. Having graduated from segregated York High in 1960, Spratt witnessed the difficult changes affecting his hometown in the 1970s.

"I was there to make compromises," Spratt said, remembering the agreement made before Dufford arrived in which African American students at Jefferson High were promised their wishes for a mascot and colors would be honored after integration. The school board didn't realize the gravity of that promise.

"The school board thought it was just a suggestion: 'We don't have to worry about it; we don't have the wherewithal to get it done.' They didn't realize the volatility of the issue and it blew up in their faces. School colors and mascot may seem trivial, but it's dead serious."

Dufford, with his ideas and enthusiasm, was met with resistance from some of York's "old guard" in the district, Spratt said.

But perhaps any superintendent receptive to full integration would have struggled in York 1 at that time. "The issue predated Bill. It was a volatile and emotional issue before he came, and it got worse when he was there. But not because of him."

Spratt remembers the "triumvirate" of Bill Dufford, Burnett Joiner, and Reed Swann, who'd taught him physics. Joiner and Swann, in particular, were important to Dufford that last year, 1976. "Without their support, I don't think Bill could have held on."

Ask Spratt if York 1's integration problems made for the roughest case in his early career, and he's fast to say no. "But it was not pleasant. It took three or four months of our time. I see Burnett or Reed or Bill from time to time and we laugh a little bit and talk about it, but we're damn glad to see it's over with."

Chapter 50

༄

The Crash

BURNETT JOINER stayed in York that summer, finishing his dissertation before moving to Orangeburg. He'd accepted a job as professor of education at South Carolina State. Working quietly one day in his office in the central administration building, he heard knocking at his door. A couple of teachers invited him to the auditorium at the high school. Entering, he found it packed. Teachers from York District 1, black and white, had filled it completely. Many had taken a day from their summer vacations so they could be there to show him their support. They said they appreciated what he had done. They asked him to stay.

"I said I couldn't, given what had happened to Dr. Dufford," Joiner said. "That was probably one of the most moving experiences I ever had, to see those teachers come out."

And so Burnett Joiner left York, where he'd never really wanted to go to in the first place, having made friendships that would last the rest of his life. Teachers and principals would call him from time to time, as he climbed higher in his career and moved farther away. His work in York, he realized later, turned out to be one of the best experiences he ever had in education. He had Bill Dufford to thank for that.

"He was probably thirty years ahead of his time in York," Joiner would say. "He took them so far in a short amount of time because of his vision for that school system and for the students. He brought them experiences they had never imagined."

But it didn't matter how much support a superintendent got from students and teachers. Board members—decision makers—would always have the final say.

"A sleeping school district emerged and was the shining star of the whole county," Joiner remembered. "People were feeling good about what was going on in York—students, parents, and the community. And it all came crashing down."

"There's no telling the accomplishments that might have been made"

Forty years after Bill Dufford left York, Nancy McFarland still wonders how the schools in District 1 might have progressed if he'd stayed. As his secretary, she watched the district take off because of his initiatives. Breakfast for hungry students, more academic programs, and an integrated high school under construction were exciting for her and her sister Betty Bigger, a longtime elementary school teacher who was one of the first to teach African American children in the district. Plus, Dufford's presence at outlying schools was a refreshing change.

"He visited the schools, ate lunch with the children, and listened to what they had to say," McFarland said. "One of the Hickory Grove children made the remark that he did not realize the district had a superintendent prior to Dr. Dufford because he had never seen him."

The needs of children came first for Dr. Dufford, and he was "unbending" in his belief that all deserved an education, McFarland recalled. He'd even asked teachers to visit their students at home.

As McFarland sees it, the all-white, all-male school board wasn't as against integration as they were for their longtime Green Dragon mascot and green and white colors. "It was something they had experienced positive results with for a long time and they didn't want to give it up." Still, she acknowledges there wasn't any board representation for the rural white and African American communities, and the promises made to Jefferson and Hickory Grove students hadn't been kept. Dufford, with his sense of fairness, clashed with a more conservative board.

"York was behind and he was advanced in his thoughts for integration," she said. "York was set in their ways."

Dufford's willingness to speak his mind and go against the status quo inspired McFarland to be more like him. "I had been one to sit in the background, stay low on the totem pole and not cause injury to myself. He encouraged me to express myself."

McFarland stayed at the district after Dufford left, working for seven superintendents during her thirty-plus years there. Dufford's two-year tenure was the most memorable.

"I feel like Dr. Dufford has given his life for the black community—that's how I feel about it," she said. "There's no telling the accomplishments that might have been made if he had been allowed to stay. But we got crossed up over colors and mascot. He was like no other superintendent we'd ever had."

Bill was principal of Edmunds High School in Sumter, South Carolina, in the late 1960s and early 1970s. He was brought in to consolidate and integrate the white high school, Edmunds, and the African American high school, Lincoln. In a 1970 yearbook photograph, Bill is sporting long sideburns. Bill recalled of an early meeting with Sumter superintendent Dr. L. C. McArthur, "He questioned the length of my sideburns. I pushed my chair back and said, 'Well, if that's all y'all need to worry about over here, I don't need to be here!'" Courtesy of Sumter County School District 1, Sumter, South Carolina.

Bill Dufford with Dr. Earl Vaughn, principal of Lincoln High School in Sumter, South Carolina, in 1969. "Our success in bringing together Edmunds and Lincoln High Schools and those students, as well as we did, would not have been possible without Earl Vaughn," Dufford recalled. "He was a great man." Courtesy of the author's collection.

These are 1970 yearbook photographs of Bill's assistant principals Reed Swann and Ethel Burnett at Edmunds High School in Sumter. "I can't say enough good things about those two leaders and their efforts to help me," Bill said. Courtesy of Sumter County School District 1, Sumter, South Carolina.

English teacher Gene Norris (far left) and Bill Dufford (far right) stand with former Beaufort High School students Julie Zachowski and Pat Conroy at the twentieth reunion of the BHS Class of 1963. Courtesy of the author's collection.

The Dufford family in 1988. Left to right: Doris, Bill, C. A. Jr., C. A. Sr., and Virginia. Courtesy of the author's collection.

Bill took this photograph of his student, friend, and celebrated writer Pat Conroy with Barbra Streisand, who directed, produced, and starred in the hit movie *The Prince of Tides* which Conroy wrote. The picture was taken at the New York film premiere in December 1991. Courtesy of the author's collection.

This photograph was taken at the December 1991 premiere of the movie *The Prince of Tides*. From left to right, Gene Norris, Conroy, and Bill. "Gene and myself were there," Bill said. "Just two country boys in the big city." Courtesy of the author's collection.

At a 1995 reunion, Gene Norris (left), Pat Conroy's Beaufort High School English teacher, and the school's secretary, Norma Duncan (right), share their memories of working together. "Gene was a unique character," Bill recalled. "He kind of adopted Pat and would take him to see southern writers up and down the South Carolina coast. And Norma was a great secretary. She never met a stranger. There are so many good things you could say about Norma." Courtesy of the author's collection.

Bill Dufford's boyhood home is now the Dufford Alumni House of Newberry College in Newberry, South Carolina. The home was given as a gift to the college by Bill and his siblings in 1998. Photograph by Ted Williams, courtesy of the Newberry Opera House.

In 2006, a group of students from Georgetown High School, where Bill was a coach, teacher, and principal during the 1950s, gathered at Libby Doggett Bernardin's house to share memories of their high school years together. Seated, from left to right, are Barbara Ward Mishoe, Libby Bernardin, Ann Thomas, and Sylvia Sawyer Owens. Standing, from left to right, are Francis "Knocky" Missroon, Danny Brabham, Betty Nelson Brown, Lula Mae Mitchum Anderson, and Bill Dufford. Courtesy of the author's collection.

In 2006, Bill Dufford was on hand to see his former student, Daisy Youngblood, presented with a celebrated MacArthur Fellowship for her work in pottery. She was a student at Beaufort High School when Bill was principal in the early 1960s. "When Daisy was at Beaufort High," Bill said, "she was my office helper." Courtesy of the author's collection.

"Walter McRackan was kind of unique to the whole story of my life," Bill said of his former student at Edmunds High School in Sumter in the late 1960s and early 1970s. "Here was a kid in the tenth grade who was probably the smartest kid in the school, but not successful academically. Walter later became president of the student body when Edmunds (the white high school) and Lincoln (the African American high school) were consolidated. When Walter saw the challenge of bringing black and white people together, he grabbed it like a dog with a bone." This photograph of McRackan was taken in 2006, courtesy of the author's collection.

Historian Alexia Helsley with her Beaufort High School English teacher, Millen Ellis, and her BHS principal, Bill Dufford, at Ellis's seventy-fifth birthday in 2013. Courtesy of the author's collection.

Bill Dufford was presented with a South Carolina Governor's Award in the Humanities on October 23, 2014. Celebrated novelist Pat Conroy, who was a student of Bill's at Beaufort High School in the 1960s, introduced him. "Pat presented me to accept the award," Bill said. "It was a great occasion. Former students and colleagues of mine from Georgetown, Beaufort, and York came. It was wonderful." Photograph by Allen Anderson, courtesy of South Carolina Humanities.

Bill received one of South Carolina's highest honors, the South Carolina Order of the Palmetto, on May 11, 2015, at the historic Newberry Opera House in Bill's hometown of Newberry. "I was very honored to receive that award on that stage," Bill said. Photograph by Ted Williams, courtesy of the Newberry Opera House.

Johnny Jones, right, was a custodian at Winyah High School in 1956. Josh Wright, left, was the custodian at Winyah Junior High School the same year. As principal at the junior high, Bill worked with Wright. "Josh was hardworking, loyal, and honorable. I can't say enough kindnesses about Josh." In 2015, Bill and several other educators would put together a celebration to honor Wright's tireless work at the school. Courtesy of Georgetown County School District, Georgetown, South Carolina.

In 2015, a memorial event was held at the historic Winyah auditorium in Georgetown, South Carolina, to honor former Winyah school custodian Josh Wright. From left to right are Nell Cribb, Jay Bazemore, and Bill—colleagues at Winyah Junior High School during the 1950s—who organized the event in honor of Wright. The portrait of Wright was created by Doug Corkern, who was a Winyah student in the 1950s. Photograph by Taylor Griffith, courtesy of the *Georgetown Times*, Georgetown, South Carolina.

Members of the Winyah High School varsity baseball team visit the old Myrtle Beach Pavilion in 1950. Bill Dufford was the team's coach as well as the school's athletics director and a teacher. "I used to take kids places. This was a Sunday afternoon. The kids didn't have anything to do, so I said, 'Let's go to Myrtle Beach.' We went in my little blue Studebaker." From left to right, Reed Swann, pitcher; Coach Dufford; Danny Brabham, center fielder; and Doug Corkern, catcher. Courtesy of the author's collection.

Seen here are the same members of the team, plus one, in a photograph taken sixty-six years later at a get-together in 2016. From left to right, pitcher Jake Lee, center fielder Danny Brabham, Coach Dufford, catcher Doug Corkern, and pitcher Reed Swann. "People in my life have tended to establish relationships that have lasted over time," Bill said. Courtesy of the author's collection.

Today Bill Dufford shares a bungalow in the Shandon neighborhood of Columbia with his house cat, Chester. "One of my former teachers from Beaufort High School was dying of cancer and wanted to make sure his cat would be taken care of, so I adopted Chester." Courtesy of the author's collection.

Bill Dufford on a Congaree River kayaking trip on October 25, 2009. From left the right: Bill Dufford, Kim Morris, Dawn Hinshaw and son Eli Latham, and Cynthia Flynn. Photograph courtesy of Michael Miller.

PART 3

∾

1977–2016

WILLIAM E. DUFFORD

Chapter 51

❧

Back Outside the Fray

WHEN I WAS MAPPING OUT MY LIFE to help write my story, the best word I could think of to describe my time in Sumter and York was "Wow." We tried to do some good things there, and we did. But as Burnett said, it all came crashing down. I wasn't angry. That's the way life was. But I was a little disillusioned.

Years after Reed, Burnett, and I left York, we heard a new athletics director and football coach had been hired for the high school. He told the board he wouldn't take the job unless they did away with the different colors and mascots for different sports. There were some new board members then, and they agreed to let the coach have his way. Guess what colors and mascot were chosen? The exact same ones our teacher group had recommended back in 1975–1976. This just shows you the power that football coaches wield in the South—and that York wasn't ready for the good work we were trying to do. They wouldn't accept the work of professional educators, but they'd listen to a football coach.

I really appreciate my friend Reed Swann. I was an outsider in York. I could leave. He had a lot more to lose. But I've been so fortunate, I need to live two lifetimes. Everyone was real good to me. I've known some real good people.

One was Joy Sovde. She was with the League of Women Voters, and her husband, Roger, was the editor of the *Rock Hill Herald*. After I left York, she asked if I'd take a job the League was involved in that had to do with fair funding for education. As the spokesperson for the Citizens' Coalition on South Carolina School Financing, I traveled around the state explaining the South Carolina Education Finance Act. The goal was to convince communities that school districts in rural or less-populated areas should be better funded, and that all children, regardless of the tax base supporting their schools, deserved an equitable education. My job was to make sure people would be informed about the law, and would vote for legislators who believed as we did. It was grassroots work, and for me, a challenge. It wasn't the kind of thing I wanted to do for the rest of my life, but it was a different way to use a moral compass. I wanted to make life better for people.

Dick Riley was elected governor in 1978, and in 1979 he appointed me co-chair of the Task Force on Southern Children. It was an outgrowth of the Southern Growth Policies Board, which Riley and Governor Jim Hunt in North Carolina had started. They were great allies. There was lots of positive leadership in the Carolinas at the time, and the Southern Growth Policies Board studied all kinds of things in eight southern states. We looked at funding for roads, needs of the poor, and education. The Task Force on Southern Children examined all kinds of things—birth rates and birth weight, ethnic diversity, teenage pregnancy, family planning, handicapped children, dental care, Medicaid, school enrollment, and school finance. Educating kids in the South, particularly when families are poor, is a complicated thing.

We published our findings in 1981. Our report was titled "Raising a New Generation in the South." I think Governor Riley hit the nail on the head in his foreword. He wrote: "The children of the South are the future of the South. Circumstances have prevented many of them from having a fair chance. We realize now that segregation 'held down' the South and precipitated problems we are still struggling to correct. Now that the process of integration is underway, there is nothing to hold us back but time and space."

It was an honor to be on the task force. I was experienced enough in education to know what needed to be studied, and there was a professional staff to research what I asked. We presented our report to the eight southern governors in hopes their legislatures would do what was recommended to bring these states forward. We had a multitude of suggestions and recommendations, and as long as we had progressive governors, we had improvement.

Integration had been and still is one of my big focuses, and the Task Force on Southern Children focused on the economically underprivileged, and how to improve the lives of kids and society in general. I was interested in all those topics, and I decided that I could be of the most service in the classroom. I don't know that many former school superintendents, with doctorates, would go back to teaching, but that was the right decision for me. I stayed in the Columbia area, teaching high school math at Eau Claire in the city and Lower Richland in the county.

Virginia, my older sister, had been teaching for years, all through integration. She would say, "You just don't know what it's like," but that didn't stop me. I had not taught for decades, until 1980. The last time I'd been a classroom teacher before then was in 1953, at Winyah High in Georgetown.

"That is the right thing to do"

Though Dick Riley never worked closely with Bill Dufford, the former governor knows the educator's stance on human rights. "He has a wonderful reputation fighting segregation and unfairness to all people, with a special interest in African Americans who had been segregated and treated unfairly," said Riley, who served as U.S. Secretary of Education after two terms as governor.

Riley appreciates Dufford's work establishing the Dufford Institute for Cultural Diversity in Newberry, equating its mission with that of the Riley Institute at Furman. "That is the right thing to do. South Carolina needs a lot of diversity training coming out of our past. He has recognized that and handled it with dignity and effectiveness. I have great respect for Bill Dufford and his name."

"He probably bought me a thousand dinners"

Tim Conroy, the second-youngest of the eight Conroy siblings, was one of many young men to rent quarters from Bill Dufford in Columbia. He was a confused USC student in 1977, on probation for two semesters in a row, when he found unexpected refuge with his oldest brother's high school principal.

"He was a father figure who did not hit. He never physically abused. He was generous and kind and passionate and talked about his feelings. He was a lot different from the Great Santini and that was really important for me in different stages of my life as I became a man."

Tim Conroy remembers when Tom, the youngest brother, moved into Dufford's upstairs apartment in 1979. Together, he and Dufford endured Tom's first bouts with schizophrenia. "I lived through that crying lots of nights in Dufford's arms, wondering what I could do, what should I do. I was frustrated and felt like I was telling people but nobody was hearing me. Dufford was so unbelievably patient."

As that difficult year continued and Tom Conroy became violent, Dufford refused to turn him out. "He hung in there and worked through what was going on," Tim Conroy said. "He was trying to figure it out along with the rest of us."

Then Dufford's upstairs flooded and Tom disappeared, panicking when the tub and shower overflowed. Tom was in tears when Dufford finally called Tim. "He still didn't want to kick him out, but I said, 'It's past time. You've done what you could do. We need to find another situation for him.'"

Life wasn't as bad for Tim Conroy as it was for Tom—who committed suicide in 1994—but it wasn't easy, either. He worked several jobs trying to make ends meet, tried several majors before finding one—education—that worked. Bill Dufford provided the constancy he needed. And the stimulation.

"There would be five or six people, often educators, sitting on his front porch talking—whether it was about politics, teaching, making an impact, getting your voice heard, racial issues, the underdog. Dufford would be animated about his feelings and especially his love for teaching."

It wasn't unusual for Dufford to invite Conroy to supper. A typical broke student, Conroy rarely refused. "He probably bought me thousands of suppers. He would literally take you out to eat. He'd say, 'You feel like seafood?' And we would leave that Edisto Avenue house and drive to Mt. Pleasant, and talk all the way down and talk all the way back. I think he always picked times when I was down, when I was depressed. He sensed I needed a little extra and he would do that."

Conroy says he's one of countless students to benefit from Dufford's generosity. "I can't describe how many people he's given money to help. It would be too long to list and he wouldn't tell you anyway. He completely does not look at life as who wins by having material possessions."

Dufford's "service over self" attitude and belief in the importance of "cultural and social connectivity" have influenced Tim Conroy deeply.

"You go into his house. There's not a lot of fancy things, not a lot of stuff he's bought for himself. He's shown me how you can really derive value and meaning from life by not having a bunch of stuff and giving back. How many people do you know who are age eighty-nine and still have friends from every generation? It's a remarkable thing about his personality."

Chapter 52

❧

The Way It Should Be

M Y SISTER VIRGINIA had thought a lot about integration, education, and children. In the 1980s, way before the idea was popular, she was suggesting uniforms to help keep discipline. She taught middle school social studies in Whitmire and Clinton, and might have been more forward-thinking than the rest of us.

C. A., my brother, experienced his own awakening. Though Dr. Grant served the black population in Newberry until about 1980, children chosen to attend the Head Start program were assigned to C. A., the town's pediatrician. Physicals were mandatory for Head Start children, but many black parents wouldn't take their kids to the doctor to get those exams. C. A. was upset to learn teachers were bringing them instead.

I said, "C. A., if you've never been to a doctor when you're black and growing up in the South, you don't know what that is. If I'm a parent and never had a chance as an adult to get a physical—particularly from a white doctor—I'm reluctant to take my kid to the doctor." It was a whole atmosphere of societal and cultural differences.

For blacks, health care during Jim Crow was difficult and scarce at best. There was no Medicare. The women who worked as maids were paid in cash, which meant there were no Social Security contributions. They couldn't get that benefit. They didn't have the money to go to the doctor. So when these parents had an opportunity to send their kids to Head Start, they didn't feel safe or comfortable. That began to get my brother to look at how things were different in the white community. I don't think he would have gathered that if he'd continued to talk to his white peers in the South. All those people were good, decent people, but they didn't understand that there had been two different societies.

During those years I was back in the classroom, I tried to think of ways to educate people about peaceful integration and the need to bring people together. My best idea was to create a center that would be devoted to diversity, and put it at a small liberal arts college in South Carolina. Both C. A. and Virginia were on the advisory committee, and so were others I'd worked with over the years—David Abel, Pat Conroy, Richard Gergel, Walter McRackan, Hayes Mizell, Dori Sanders, Jim Solomon. We named it the Dufford Diversity Center, and we were going to start it with $1 million.

Naturally we approached Newberry College first. My siblings and I had already donated our family home to the college, thinking it would make a fine president's house. When they didn't accept our offer for the institute, we started casting about for others. The president at the College of Charleston was very interested; they had just started a program for Jewish studies. But that president left, and the new president wasn't interested. Eventually we got about twenty-three proposals and it had gotten competitive. The group that made the best proposal was the Humanities Council[SC], but they and we realized, after talking about it, that their staff was too small to take it on.

Diversity as a concept hadn't caught on yet, but Bernie Dunlap, the president of Wofford, was excited about it. So were the people at Francis Marion University. We went to Bernie's office, and he made a great proposal. Then Deborah Smith with the Newberry Opera House made a proposal at the last minute. We were getting committee fatigue. And my thought was, "Here is the Dufford family, who attempted to give this institute to Newberry College, who had been in Newberry since 1923." It saddened me that we were going to move this to Wofford.

By then all of my siblings had passed away. When Deborah made the proposal, we said, "Let's keep it in Newberry." We changed our concept to something more compatible with the opera house, and now we're teaching young children about diversity instead of college students. Our name changed too. The Dufford Institute for Cultural Diversity started in 2010.

Those children come to cultural programs at the opera house at least every month. And every year we have a special program about segregation and integration. We usually have that program during Dufford Diversity and Inclusion Week, a program Newberry College presents every October. We have lectures, panel discussions, luncheons, and breakfasts, all pertaining to diversity and fairness. Some of our speakers have been Congressman James Clyburn, Shannon Faulkner, the first woman cadet at the Citadel, Justin Machado, a writer/producer for Bounce TV, the Reverend Mark Adams, a Presbyterian minister who works on the border between the United States and Mexico, and Pastor Dermon Sox Jr. In 2013, for the first Dufford Diversity and Inclusion Week, I invited some of my former students from Edmunds High to talk to the college students.

In 2014, Reed Swann, Burnett Joiner, Moses Rabb, and I participated in the program we had for children at the opera house. We sat on the stage while third graders watched. Timmy Conroy, who'd just retired from teaching special education, was our announcer. We showed the children how things used to be. When we talked about the Jim Crow South, Reed and I—the white guys—sat together. Burnett and Moses—our black friends—sat together, apart from us.

Then we put all our chairs together, and the children saw four men, black and white, sitting close together.

That's the way it should be.

"These little minds are wide open"

It's become a common sight in twenty-first-century Newberry: elementary school children excitedly dragging their hesitant parents by the hand to the grandly restored Newberry Opera House. More than likely, the children and parents are Hispanic, reflecting a very different Newberry from the Depression-era, black-and-white town Bill Dufford knew as a child. Those children and parents—as well as their African American and white counterparts—are the fortunate recipients of Dufford's largess. The children in particular, the Dufford Scholars, receive three years of broadening performances and accompanying classroom lessons. That's a surface definition of what the Dufford Institute for Cultural Diversity provides.

"It has been incredibly successful," said Deborah Smith, founding director of the Newberry Opera House. "The students' eyes have opened, and they're so much more aware of what is going on around them. Their vocabulary is changing."

The Dufford Institute for Cultural Diversity wasn't Bill Dufford's original concept. He envisioned a "Dufford Diversity Center" at a college, preferably Newberry College, his alma mater. Having struck out there and at other colleges and organizations, he found himself in a random conversation with Smith.

"He came by one afternoon and told me he was about to head up to Wofford to talk to them about his project and he and I started talking about it and decided, 'What the heck, why not put it here?'" Smith recalled. "He was thinking of college students, and we have found together that the impact is incredible with younger kids. Your chance of catching a child and changing his attitude diminishes the older they get. These little minds are wide open. They are curious and interested and want to take in everything we have to offer. And they are nonjudgmental. They just look at the world and figure, 'Okay, that's the way it is, what do we do with it?' It's not negative. It's a starting place, and they want to make the world theirs. And that's about as good an attitude of any you can have."

In 2015, the first class of Dufford Scholars—all 340 of them—graduated from the program. Scholars start in the third grade and continue through fifth, allowing plenty of in-depth time to soak up important life lessons. Besides performing for them in the opera house once a month, the artists visit them in their classrooms. On the evenings of the daytime performances, the students come back for a variation of the same performance, often with their parents. All public school third graders in the district participate, including the Newberry schools of Dufford's childhood: Speers Street, Boundary Street, and Gallman. Education packets are created and distributed for every performance, and teacher orientations are given every year. Dufford Scholars are involved with opera house programs three of four weeks a month.

The daytime programs are interactive, with musicians and dancers talking to the students and answering questions. Many of the performers speak Spanish and English, and children are called to the stage to translate both languages. Most programs point to a world outside Newberry—dance troupes from Siberia and Brazil, musicians from Cuba, Mexico, and Celtic regions, acrobats from Shanghai. Others are more local, with South Carolina storytellers and a Civil War drama. There have been science lessons, such as the Bella Gaia environmental awareness program, which focuses on climate change and global unity, and which features photos taken mainly from the International Space Station while musicians and dancers perform. A 2015 program gave the Dufford Scholars a chance to hear from surviving members of the Friendship Nine from Rock Hill when the group came to Newberry to talk about their 1961 sit-in and its role in the history of the civil rights movement.

Three programs have been particularly well-received. A beach music program featuring Harry Turner, Little Caesar, Clay Brown, and the late Billy Scott had children shagging in the schools and learning the music is rooted in African American culture. Newberry native and dancer Terrance Henderson and the members of the Dance Theatre of Harlem stressed the message that persistence and years of hard work pay off.

"I think it's a message that cannot be told enough," Smith said. "You have to reinforce to these kids they can do anything. These dancers were judged on skill—not that they came from a little town in North Dakota or North, South Carolina. They loved dance, they didn't want to do anything but dance, and they practiced for hours after school, and sacrificed. And that's the way you become a dancer. Or an astronaut, or president."

An unforeseen benefit is that Dufford Scholars learn proper performance etiquette. "They know how to act, how to dress, when to stand up and clap and when not to, and what it means when the lights dim," Smith said. "They very quickly learn the opera house is theirs. When I go to Walmart, I'll hear, 'Hey Miss Smith,' and it will be one of my Dufford kids. They have claimed ownership of the staff too."

A retired school principal is the institute's liaison with the schools; the district superintendent is on the Opera House's board of directors.

"We know the kids enjoy this program and we are hoping to be able to show specific benefits they derive from it," said Phil Astwood, a retired USC professor who has been evaluating the program. "It is clear, however, that were it not for this program, most of these students would never see a ballet, hear *Porgy and Bess*, or have the chance to get up on a stage and dance to live Cuban music."

Through the Dufford Institute for Cultural Diversity, Bill Dufford has given the children of Newberry a positive and lasting gift, Smith said.

"These kids would not have had the opportunity had it not been for Bill Dufford, and this opportunity is truly changing their lives. His vision is astounding, and he follows through on his vision, which is a pretty wonderful thing. The Dufford Institute is a program the opera house will be known for in the years to come, more than our programming. If we can make a difference in the lives of ten or fifteen kids, much less three hundred, how lucky we are."

"It was like somebody stabbed me"

There are so many things Leighton Cubbage will never forget about 1969–1970. Probably the best part of "The Dufford Year"—a name he coined years later, after he'd reflected upon it as an adult—was winning the 1969 state football championship. Bill Dufford stood on the sidelines with the team as Edmunds beat Gaffney. For Cubbage, a junior, the victory meant so much more than the banquets, gifts, and Peach Bowl parade that followed. Winning every game of a season, plus the championship, taught him winning is possible to begin with.

"That changed my life. I believe I can win them all, because I've experienced it."

Cubbage also is the one who compared The Dufford Year to Camelot. An outstanding student body and forward-thinking faculty, led by a "joyful" chief who worked well with coaches and staff, made Edmunds High a pleasurable place to be, despite the difficulty of the times. Dufford's "raw leadership" made it so, Cubbage believes.

"Some of that tension and natural apprehension of putting blacks and whites together—humor and laughter moved that aside. He was just as likely to have his arm around a black person as a white person. He was the leader who leads from the front; he wasn't hidden behind his desk and paperwork. He was in the halls, he was at the games, he was at the plays, he was wide open."

A successful businessman in Greenville, Cubbage recognizes now that Dufford's attitude of joy, happiness, love, and inclusivity is what makes organizations work best. "That's the right type of fuel to drive any kind of culture. People can talk about that ideal inside a church or in a pew, but there's a guy who had the courage to do it inside a *school*. It could have been like fire hitting wood, it could have exploded. But he diffused and transcended that with his attitude and the way he treated people. It's really quite remarkable."

When Dufford invited Cubbage to participate in a panel discussion during Dufford Diversity Week at Newberry College in 2013, he automatically accepted. The people at his office were incredulous that their sixty-year-old boss was leaping to do whatever his high school administrator asked. "But that's the power of a leader," he explained to the Newberry students. "That's what somebody will do when that person makes a difference in your life. He's the first white guy I ever saw in my life who was worried about what was going to happen to a black kid. That's why our high school was different."

Cubbage was a senior after Dufford left Sumter, and to him it seemed as if Camelot crumbled. During that first year of full integration—1970–1971—many of his white classmates transferred to private schools. Cubbage thought those students were "cowards," that they should stay where they were, fix the problems so their own kids wouldn't have to go through what they were going through. Meanwhile, African American juniors and seniors who'd been at Lincoln High were now at the newly named Sumter High, creating practically a new student body. And students once again were in the "prison-inmate" atmosphere as before. Cubbage, senior class president of the mostly white Edmunds High, became co-president with Larry Blanding, elected from Lincoln. Cubbage and Blanding were on the two student councils who negotiated their new school's colors, mascot, and name. It was like two planets colliding, so segregated their worlds had been, Cubbage described.

"It was surreal," he told the Newberry students. "I see the smiles on the faces of people in this room. We're like people from outer space talking about an era that was bizarre and things you can't even fathom. But sitting here in 2013, I thank God we went through what we went through so y'all don't have to."

Cubbage compares being a student leader and athlete that Dufford Year to being like Forrest Gump. Like it or not, you were in a certain place at a certain time when great change was coming, and you had to act, you had to make important decisions. He knew he'd much rather be doing what he thought he'd be doing in high school—hanging out with friends, getting a date, playing sports. Dealing with three hundred years of history and volatile political beliefs was not something he planned or wanted. But he'd played football with two star African American teammates, and there was something about winning, losing, getting hurt, and bleeding with someone of any color wearing the same uniform you were. Besides, he couldn't forget C. A. Wilson telling him about being chased and called "nigger."

"It was like somebody stabbed me," Cubbage said. "That one moment was when I realized inside of each person is a unique heart."

Chapter 53

◞◉◟

Justice and Fairness

Now that i'm retired, I've had time to think about things, to really reflect on my life and on all the people who have been a part of my story—who are still a part of my story. We really have a lot more work to do in this country if we're to get it right as best we can. These riots in Ferguson and Baltimore and the police shooting deaths of young black men that gave rise to the Black Lives Matter movement tell me white people still haven't accepted black people as equal members of our shared society. People think we need to do away with Affirmative Action. They ask, "How long are we going to give in to these African Americans?" My answer is, "As long as we kept them from joining society—hundreds of years. Let's give them that amount of time."

People are stunned when I say that. But I tell them, "If you have to ask the question, you're not feeling the pain for those who've been mistreated." They wouldn't be asking the question, they'd be saying, "Let's just get on with this." We've got to get to a level playing field, and we're not there yet.

I am convinced the problem with integration was among the white population. The black population was receptive to improving education for their kids. The problem was the white kids and what they were hearing from their parents. If you can get the white kids to accept people who are different from them, there's a great deal more possibility for success. But kids model what they see and hear at home.

The black kids never were a problem in the initial step toward integration. It was the action of white kids, white parents, white school boards, and white superintendents that caused blockage and caused blacks to become more vocal. When you're told you're not supposed to be here and you know you are by law, you begin to behave a little differently. We should be able to expect fairness, equality, and kindness in our lives, but when entire races of people can't get that in a country founded on the principle that "all men are created equal," then we have a problem that can only be solved by all of us working together to bring everybody along.

In Ms. Vaden's dissertation, she wrote about specific instances around the state of resistance to integration by white kids, parents, school boards, and superintendents. And she wrote about the actions of black students, parents, and civil rights leaders faced with unlawful ill treatment, disrespect, and disparity in the public schools.

For instance, in rural Dorchester County, in August 1969, Four Holes School was a four-room concrete building serving an isolated community called "Four Holes" because of its proximity to the Four Holes Swamp. Ms. Vaden wrote that the school was also called the "Indian School" because the small group of children who attended were of Native American, African, and European descent.

Late that summer, the children of Four Holes School, their parents, and civil rights leaders went to nearby Ridgeville Elementary School, in Ridgeville, to demand that the Four Holes children be enrolled there. Ridgeville Elementary was much bigger. It was staffed with certified teachers. There were music and art programs available. Ms. Vaden wrote that when the Four Holes contingent arrived at Ridgeville Elementary, it was met by the Dorchester County school superintendent and some Ridgeville faculty members holding signs directing "all Indians to the gymnasium." The superintendent told the adults and children from Four Holes School that Ridgeville's classrooms were overcrowded and couldn't hold any more students, when, in fact, the classrooms there were less crowded than the ones at Four Holes School.

Ms. Vaden also wrote about two hundred black students walking out of Rock Hill High School in January 26, 1972. The students were already angry about racially discriminatory policies and the firing and demotion of their favorite black coaches after desegregation. But when the Rock Hill High band director forced black students to play "Dixie," that was the straw that broke the camel's back. Two hundred black students walked out of that school.

You see, white people were just keeping black people down. If I'd been kept down for years and years, I don't know that I wouldn't have reacted the same way. But white people don't often think about what it might be like to be anything other than white. There's an empathy there that's missing, and we need to foster it.

What went on in Ferguson, Missouri, in 2014—an unarmed black teenager being shot and killed by a white police officer—that kid didn't need to get killed. Those nine people at Emanuel AME Church in Charleston didn't need to get killed either. It's horrible what happened there on June 17, 2015. And it's a shame it took that act of terrorism to get the state legislature to take down the Confederate flag at the statehouse. I can't help but remember how the faculty at Edmunds High School unanimously decided to take that flag down in 1969. In 1969! We knew it was divisive then. That faculty realized we were faced with the process of bringing black and white people together and they voted to do away with any symbolism of separation of the races. Almost fifty years later, people are starting to realize the same thing. What a great tribute to that forward-thinking faculty, and what a shame that so many others are just now catching up to that kind of thinking and acting for the common good.

We've been misled into thinking our problems with race are over because Barack Obama got elected to the presidency. But they're not over. We might get a Muslim president one day. Our responsibilities for gender equality are not over either, for that matter.

People think one person will come through to change things, and I think so often that that hope is irrelevant. You have to look at how we bring people together with justice and fairness and equality and then you can say, "We made it, *we* made it," rather than waiting for one person. We need to give people a chance.

My skin tells me I've been on the top side of this. But we've got a long way to go for justice and fairness for black people, women, and all people who aren't of the privileged class of Jim Crow.

"One World, One People"

When Lawton Swann was trying to figure out whether to get a master's degree in education at USC, it was only natural Bill Dufford would play a part in his decision. Reed and Hunter Swann's son grew up hearing stories about integration since his childhood in Barnwell. For Lawton, "Doc" was practically a family member.

Still, Lawton was unsure about whether to pursue a career in education. He worked as a teacher's assistant in Columbia, renting from Dufford, before realizing his parents' calling was also his own. Long talks on the couch with his landlord helped solidify his decision.

"We weren't doing enough to understand the differences in the communities, in the African American community," Lawton said. "The big thing is you have a lot of white teachers who can't understand that the reason students perform differently or behave differently is because of their culture and how they were raised. Hearing those stories about Lincoln and Edmunds helped me understand how kids sometimes know a lot more about how to fix the issue than adults. The people who think they're so smart—sometimes those people can get in the way."

By the time Lawton earned his master's in elementary education in 2006, he'd also gotten an education in politics. Dufford ushered him to a showing of *The Corridor of Shame*, the documentary about South Carolina's neglected public schools, and they participated in a march at the statehouse. The importance of public education was always at the forefront of their conversations, but so was tolerance for all people.

"He lives this lifestyle—one world, one people. We're much more alike than we're different. Race, religion, gender, sexual orientation—those types of descriptors typically used as reasons why somebody should be feared or not accepted by a vast majority of our population—those things are what make us great. In the midst of all the hate that seemed to be put on the Muslim and Islamic people in our country, Doc was always talking about how we should be more accepting and kind and try to understand the differences in people."

Lawton taught fourth grade for six years in Richland District 2 and now is a technology integration specialist in Lexington District 1. He inherited his father's love for radio and hosts a sports show. Like other Dufford tenants, he has favorite memories. "I'd come in from school and the cats were always sitting with him. Bomber and Dinkins were loyal to the core. Bomber may have been the most politically involved feline in the country. He was always locked in watching TV with Doc."

Also like others, Lawton marvels at the friends Dufford has made, including many who work at the restaurants where he eats breakfast and supper. "They're so familiar with him they have his water to go. He's not going to have to ask for that. For a guy who doesn't have any children, and being the only surviving member of his family, he sure does have a big family."

Chapter 54

༽

The Old Plantation and the Upper Room

I SUGGESTED TO AÏDA ROGERS that she should read Luci Vaden's dissertation. Miss Vaden interviewed me for part of it, but I didn't know she'd learned what she did until I read what she wrote. I was stunned, reading it. I am stunned that a lot of my professional colleagues were doing such mean-spirited things. They were breaking the law, but loved to tell you, "I'm a good Christian and I love to abide by the law, and if these black folks don't abide by the law, we need to shoot 'em." Some of the people mentioned in that dissertation are people I knew from Newberry College.

That dissertation made me realize we were doing some good things in Sumter and York. Obviously we were if we were invited to Tuscaloosa and Boston to help other school districts. But we didn't have a blueprint; we were just coming up with ideas.

I was pretty lucky that things were peaceful in Georgetown in the 1950s and in Beaufort in the 1960s. But they weren't in Orangeburg. In that county, ninety-two blacks petitioned the school board to desegregate in 1955. The mayor of Elloree said, "We will fight the leaders of the NAACP from ditches to fence posts to keep Negroes out of white schools." The white people in the county and elsewhere in the state started White Citizens Councils, and the one in Elloree got eight hundred members in its first week.

Then in 1956 the state legislature made it illegal for a school district to hire or employ a member of the NAACP. Teachers had to submit a "written oath" they weren't members. If they didn't complete a questionnaire about whether they were, they could be fired. Twenty-one teachers at Elloree County Training School, an all-black school, were fired for refusing to complete that questionnaire. Think about how crazy that was.

In 1970, when I was in Sumter, more than one hundred white students attacked nineteen black students at Harleyville-Ridgeville High School in Dorchester County. Teachers didn't even help the black students. It was said some teachers even encouraged the fight. Three black girls were hurt bad enough to go to the hospital, but did any of the white students get punished? No. But three black students were suspended.

I didn't know a lot of this until I read Miss Vaden's report. What I did know was that Freedom of Choice wasn't enough for true integration. There was a plantation mentality about that, particularly when it came to teachers. The black teachers did whatever the white school boards wanted, and if the board decided a black teacher needed to move to a white school, there were no questions asked. Those decisions weren't discussed openly. There were systems of communicating where white people found out who the good black teachers were. It was like, "Ms. Wright or Ms. Jones over there has good qualifications. She's been to Peabody College; she didn't get her degree from South Carolina State. We'll move her over here."

You think the white school board is going to put an inferior black teacher over there among the white kids? They were making their decisions and they were up in the Upper Room. Isn't that kind of biblical? They were doing it all in the Upper Room, the boardroom.

Black teachers couldn't contest their assignments. But teachers, black and white, were passive. They were making minimum wage and unwilling to join a union and shake up the system.

But you have to remember, sometimes the school teacher was the family breadwinner. She's going to go where there's an income promised. Being a school teacher in South Carolina was usually the best job an African American could get. We had no dental school for blacks; we had no law school.

And there was a status-type thing to being a black school teacher chosen to teach in a white school. That teacher would think, "Ah, I must be pretty important." It's all mixed up. It's all mixed up.

Chapter 55

ᶜ⤳

Oldest Living Newberry Indian

EARLIER, Lawton Swann mentioned my cats Bomber and Dinkins, littermates I got in 1989. They were terrific cats, both of whom passed away a few years ago. Now I have Chester, and we still do a lot of television watching, that ornery cat and I. We keep it on the cable news channels. In the coverage from around the world, it's easy to see some progress has been made in terms of integration, but an awful lot of stuff has been driven underground. How can I say this? You can't legislate making people love one another. You don't need to love anybody, but you need to recognize that everyone is entitled to the same benefits that everybody else gets.

Aïda asked me how I felt about same-sex marriage. I told her I've changed about that too. I was brought up with the belief that marriage is to be between a man and a woman, but marriage is love and the way people love one another. I think two men can love one another and two women can love one another. Do you deny them the same rights and benefits of marriage between a man and woman? Marriage equality for same-sex partners is not going to destroy the world, I'm telling you.

Some people think that when older people die, their prejudices will too. But we have to remember they influence their kids, and talk radio will influence the way people think. White people will look at things from a white perspective and black people will look at things from a black perspective. We've got to look at it as all-inclusive. If we're going to make progress in the world, we've got to bring it together, some way. We can't do this separately. Like the '54 decision said, separate is inherently unequal.

Of course, we've got to be inclusive to all the races. Let's take what happened at Newberry College around 2005. I took a very strong position that we needed to do away with the Indian mascot. I thought it was degrading to Native Americans and the faculty did too. The faculty even passed a unanimous resolution that the Indian as a mascot didn't fit with the college's mission statement or its Christian founding and teaching. They presented their resolution to the board of trustees, and the board refused to act upon the resolution.

While other institutions of higher education—like Stanford University and Marquette University—had realized the injury caused by using Native Americans as mascots, the Newberry College president and board fought diligently to keep the Indian as our mascot. It's an emotional issue, and they stirred people up, just like what we went through in Sumter and York. But we were in the midst of a national movement on this issue. When the Tusculum College football team from East Tennessee came to play Newberry in 1989, several Native American students came with them to protest the Newberry mascot. And when I say protest, what I really mean is to educate our students. They handed out pamphlets outlining why the use of Native Americans as sports mascots was inherently racist, and it got me to thinking about the subject in a new light. I was on the college's board of trustees at the time, and I remember taking one of those pamphlets to our new college president at that game and telling him we needed to have a look at this. Well, you can imagine how well that went over!

So I got forty-two pages of research from Stanford University, which has an excellent Native American Studies program, and I shared it with the college's board. The truth is, there's no reason why Newberry College should have an Indian as its mascot. There is no Native American connection to our school or our town. Here's how we really got that mascot in the first place: in the early 1900s, Newberry College's baseball team wore red uniforms. They were cast-offs from a semi-professional textile team. Then in the press, someone wrote, "Here come the Red Men," and that evolved into "Indians." Our only connection is through old red baseball uniforms. This is the craziest thing in the world!

Anyway, the NCAA agreed with Native Americans that using the Indian as a mascot was wrong. They pressured colleges to change if they wanted to remain in the NCAA. Newberry College appealed at first, and then finally agreed in 2010. Our mascot is the wolf now.

What they could have done as an institution of higher learning—knowing Native Americans were upset by being used in that manner and with a faculty 100 percent supportive of not using humans as mascots—is gone out and made a great thing of abiding with the NCAA directive against Native American-themed mascots. Their explanation could have been very noble, that changing the mascot fit right in with the mission and the Christian creed of the college. But to this day, there are white people who claim with pride that they still are Newberry Indians.

It didn't serve me personally to do away with the mascot. As a Newberry College batboy, ballboy, and player, I'm the oldest living "Indian" around. But I'm on the side of the NCAA and Native Americans because of a sense of fairness. Native Americans don't want to be put in a category with cats and dogs and tigers and gamecocks. They deserve respect.

It's so important to me that Newberry College officials recognize the value of fairness that I've paid to send coaches and athletes to learn more about the civil rights struggle. When the Citadel put on a conference about civil rights, I paid for the assistant coaches to go so they could get some sensitivity training. It really bothered me that we had an all-white football staff—including the coach and assistant coaches—and mostly black players.

It took them a while to hire a black assistant coach. Not long after that, I helped finance the basketball team's trip to Washington, D.C. They were invited to play up there but didn't have the money to go. I told the coach, Dave Davis, I'd help them get there, but the only thing I wanted in return was a picture of the team at the Martin Luther King Jr. memorial. And do you know, they did what I asked. I've got the picture and the coach made each of the players write me a thank-you note. I got a kick out of that. Two of the players were white boys from Nova Scotia. Most of the rest of the team were African American.

What I'm getting at is this: it's very important the way you treat people. People probably won't remember what you said and they probably won't remember what you did, but they will remember how you made them feel. That's a pretty important philosophy.

"A restless discomfort for injustice"

"By my light I enlighten" is the translation of *Luceo Mea Luce*, the name of the award Newberry College faculty members give for distinguished service. Bill Dufford received the honor in 2004, no doubt for decades of loyalty to his alma mater. But it may be that Dufford began enlightening others in his hometown most overtly and effectively in 2013 when Newberry College presented its first Dufford Diversity and Inclusion Week.

Prom Night in Mississippi, a documentary about a town finally integrating its junior-senior in 2007, heralded the first Dufford Diversity and Inclusion Week. That week also featured Shannon Faulkner, the Citadel's first female cadet; and a discussion of Bill Dufford's Sumter experiences with a panel including Moses Rabb, Reed Swann, Allen Johnson, Leighton Cubbage, and Barney Shorter. Since then, several well-known speakers on civil rights and diversity history and education—including U.S. Congressman James E. Clyburn, surviving members of the Friendship Nine, filmmaker Bud Ferillo, and attorney Carl Epps (one of Bill Dufford's stand-out students from Beaufort)—have addressed students, faculty, staff, and community members in panel discussions, breakfasts, and luncheons. In conjunction with Newberry College, the Newberry Opera House offers a diversity-related performance during the week. In 2015, *No Fear for Freedom: The Musical* was presented. Based on a children's book by Kimberly P. Johnson, it chronicles the story of the Friendship Nine, the Friendship Junior College students in Rock Hill who were jailed trying to integrate McCrory's lunch counter in 1961.

"At Newberry College we want our students to have a restless discomfort for injustice, oppression and the exploitation of people," said Dr. Maurice Scherrens, the college's twenty-second president. "We want our students to understand the past and be passionate about taking action to build an environment where there is justice, freedom, and peace among all constituents. Dufford Diversity Week heightens awareness, and as a college and a community we use that awareness to bring about change."

Anywhere from sixty to more than a hundred people attend the presentations, and Dufford makes a point to talk to the students. "He has such a keen memory of historical events, and the stories he shares with the students are so very interesting," said Dr. Peggy B. Winder, a professor in the college's Department of Sport Professions and the director of diversity education. "It's one thing to read about past diversity-related events, but Dr. Dufford has lived through many of these events, which makes it more meaningful for many of our students."

Attending the lectures and presentations isn't a requirement for students, though some get a Fine Arts and Lectures credit. "Many students just come because they know the event will be educational and of great interest," Winder said.

A quote from Dufford in 1969 anchors the program. "We must respect the dignity of the past, but know and respect the fact that our past means different things to different people." That quote appears on Dufford Diversity materials and informs the spirit of discovery and empathy that will be represented in programs to be taught in the Dufford Diversity Lab, a new classroom within the Speers Street Elementary School. The school, which Dufford attended as a boy, is the college's new home for its Department of Teacher Education and Sport Professions. Ground was broken for its revitalization in May 2015.

Scherrens, Newberry College president since August 2012, appreciates Dufford's open mind and generous character. "We can create a softer and more empathetic world if we are willing to understand and appreciate the views of those who are different than us," he said. "It is one of our institutional beliefs that as a people we gain strength as a community as we better understand the perspectives of others."

"Everybody's important"

In the early 1990s, the boys on the Seven Oaks Presbyterian Church basketball team in Columbia had an unusual pair of coaches. Langston Spotts, a USC student in his early twenties, was head coach. His assistant? Sixty-five-year-old Bill Dufford. For Spotts, who was renting Dufford's upstairs apartment at the time, it was brilliant and logical to ask his landlord to help him. Dufford had the time and experience, and he'd even coached his own father. Phil Spotts had grown up in Newberry and become a high school coach, principal, and administrator.

"He has a natural knack for communicating with young people," Spotts said, recalling how the players responded to Dufford's friendly ribbing. "He would say things to get a smile on their face, and they'd think, 'I can talk to this guy. He's real. And I'm going to listen to him.' But we took it seriously. We wanted to win." Spotts and Dufford coached one of their teams to Columbia's YMCA church league championship.

Spotts was probably the age of the players he was coaching—a high school freshman at Irmo—when he met Dufford the first time during a chance run-in with his father. At a second encounter, again with his father, Dufford asked young Spotts about his interests. Learning he loved basketball and was a fan of former USC player Alexander English, Dufford invited him to attend the basketball camp the NBA star sponsored at Newberry College. Spotts was a little tongue-tied when he met English. Reflecting later, it was the invitation that mattered more.

"It was very neat to meet Alex English, but that Dr. Dufford took the time to do that for me was very impressive."

Bill Dufford would do a lot more for Spotts over the years. During his six years as his tenant, through undergraduate and graduate school, Spotts felt his mind sharpening. After a night out, Spotts would be home in time to watch the news with Dufford.

"That was the first time I began to analyze things more and ask questions. He had a way of being curious that I can relate to, and he would challenge me. I learned how to think for myself and not accept things at face value, and that came from night-in, night-out watching the news with him."

Education, government, and the environment were regular topics. Because Spotts was working on a master's degree in health administration, health care was another. Spotts and Dufford didn't always agree. "He was very committed to his principles, which I admired so much. There were times I felt as strongly, but it was interesting to hear his position. He could always support his position, and that, to me, was what was so thought-provoking. He made me open-minded to both sides."

While conversations could be serious at home, Dufford's light teasing in public always made him fun company. "Whenever he would introduce me to somebody that knows my father, he would typically say, 'This is Phil Spotts's son, but don't hold that against him.' That would make the other person smile and break the ice."

Similar incidents would occur at restaurant cash registers. "When the person would ask how the meal was, he'd say, 'The meal was great. The company wasn't too good.' And I would smile and they would smile."

Funny remarks to strangers might not seem important, but Spotts has learned they are. "It was the way he would try to relate to somebody or communicate with someone, and it would make that person smile for a moment. I learned that lesson from him. I'm not as outgoing as he is, but I learned that skill and use it in appropriate situations."

As CEO for Columbia Eye Clinic, Spotts has learned that showing an interest in employees—and everyone—is critical. "Watching him skillfully communicate with people and break the ice during a random encounter—that was a message to me that everybody's important. Whether it's your boss, the person checking you out at a restaurant, or if you're at a company and there's a new employee, everybody is important and you should get to know them and take advantage of the opportunity to put a smile on their face."

"The straw that stirred the drink"

Taking a long, measured look back at Bill Dufford's life, Danny Brabham compares him to one of America's greatest baseball players. "If I could use Reggie Jackson's theme song, he was 'the straw that stirred the drink.' Dufford walking into different situations was the straw that stirred the drink to get people to do what they had to do to come together."

Brabham was sixteen when he first met Bill Dufford, and they remain close friends to this day. A 1952 Winyah High graduate, Brabham had Dufford as his basketball and baseball coach and trigonometry and physics teacher. Brabham took Dufford's path, graduating from Newberry College and then coaching and teaching math and science at high schools in Rock Hill, Spartanburg, Cheraw, and Myrtle Beach. As a fellow educator—Brabham also worked in county and state education administration—he can profess to Dufford's natural gifts at all levels of schooling. Dufford was necessarily authoritative as a teacher and coach, as well as a good listener and delegator as a principal.

Dufford's work in Georgetown, Beaufort, and Sumter allowed him to experience different kinds of students from a variety of backgrounds during changing times, which in turn made him a better educator. From all-white segregated students to frequently uprooted, worldly military students to black and white teens grappling with integration, Dufford learned from his various environments and improved himself.

"He grew more and more, and going to the University of Florida and getting his doctorate opened his eyes in terms of what was happening, and it made him a better person," Brabham said. "He saw the dynamics of change."

He also realized collaborating on a problem was better than trying to solve it alone. "Each of us don't have the answer to every problem, but collectively, when you get your minds together, you solve the problems together. He's used the advantage of working with other people to talk about what we needed to do and used what they suggested."

As important as reaching out to African Americans was his outreach to whites, Brabham observed. "He helped those of another race understand how important it was to give everybody equal opportunity."

Dufford's interest in helping "the underdog" was evident even during his earliest years in Georgetown. "We had three groups of kids—downtown, out of town, and mill kids. This is true in every town. When you talk about blue collars and working hard and different backgrounds, Bill Dufford had the heart to help those who needed help."

Brabham calls himself one who didn't have every advantage. His father grew up in Epworth Orphanage in Columbia; both parents worked, neither finished high school. It was Bill Dufford who drove Brabham to Newberry College to meet Coach Harvey Kirkland, for whom he'd play quarterback. Once enrolled, Brabham visited Dufford's family frequently. "They were like my home away from home."

Coach John Hutchison at Cheraw High once told Brabham something he never forgot: "'Danny, there are five people you can count on to come to your rescue. The rest are just friends.' You can count on Dufford. He has that character that he's going to help you if you get in trouble."

Chapter 56

❧

Houses and Kids and Cars

JEFFREY GREENE finished Beaufort High School in 1964 during my tenure as principal. Jeff was a model student. At the time of his graduation, the Vietnam War was in full swing. Jeff was not necessarily in favor of the war, but as a faithful and dutiful youngster, he served his time. After all, his father was a career Marine.

After honorably serving his country, Jeff decided to pursue his higher education. In 1970 he enrolled at USC in Columbia. That's the same year, after leaving Sumter, that I had accepted a teaching position as a staff member of the Center for Integrated Education at USC. I had rented a two-bedroom apartment and I needed someone to keep the place neat and to cook. (I never had to cook because of the availability of school cafeterias.) Jeff needed financial help and I needed nourishment. It was a perfect fit.

During that time, Billy Jones, another one of my former students from Beaufort, Class of '59, was an agent for Russell Jeffcoat Realty. Billy called one day to see if I was interested in "expanding my portfolio." My response was, "Oh, I lay awake at night worrying about my portfolio." I really didn't know what he was talking about. But Billy ended up selling me a duplex apartment on Princess Street and a house on South Edisto Avenue, both in Columbia, and a house in Cayce on New State Road, which Aïda wrote about earlier. This gave me space to fill! Soon there were former students of mine from Beaufort and Sumter, as well as sons of former students from Georgetown, all staying in these places.

Jeff was always right there, keeping everyone in order and basically supervising the younger college students. Jeff was kind and generous, but we all knew who "the boss" was. During this time, Jeff met a young girl who was a student in an independent study course I was teaching, Elizabeth Townsend, who Jeff later married, and they are still happily together after all of these years.

After graduating from USC, Jeff worked with PBS *Radio Reader* at Michigan State University. He later became a textbook editor at Houghton Mifflin and eventually retired to Concord, Massachusetts.

In retirement, he takes continuing education courses at Harvard, including one in poetry.

When Jeff called me just after the historic flooding in South Carolina in October 2015, he was finishing his course in poetry. Inspired by what was happening in South Carolina, he wrote the poem that appears at the front of this book as his tribute to our longtime friendship and mutual respect. Jeff has been a great presence in my life, and I appreciate his friendship and his poetry. Having former students like Jeff stay in my life has been part of the great, continuous circle of my experiences in education, well beyond the halls, classrooms, gyms, and ball fields of schools, and it has been my privilege to see so many grow into good, wonderful people.

But let me tell you something else about Jeff Greene. He wrecked my car! It's funny what kids remember. Some of them seem to make a big deal out of my cars. I've been buying cars for fifty years. I keep them for eight years. I've had a Mazda, a Volvo, a Chrysler, some Plymouths, a Peugeot. I never felt too possessive about material things. When I was at Lower Richland, I had a kid who needed a car to go to his junior-senior. If it's a responsible person, what's wrong with that? I lent him my car.

Well, two kids wrecked my cars. The first was Bruce Byrum, a student from Beaufort, who was the manager of the University of Florida baseball team when I was getting my doctorate at Florida. We'd drive back home together for Christmas and vacation. One time we had an accident in Augusta. He was driving, and he felt so bad about it. Bruce later became a general in the Marine Corps, another of my accomplished students who stays in touch.

Then when Jeff Greene was renting a room from me in Columbia, he'd use my car to go shopping for our groceries. I got a call one day; he said my car's been in an accident. That was a beautiful car Jeff wrecked, a Plymouth Sport Fury—sable white with a red stripe down the side and a black vinyl top. I saw it in an ad and went to the dealer and asked them to order it.

But so what? They aren't nothing but cars. And nobody was hurt. These were responsible kids, and they've become remarkable adults. You've got to do something for somebody else somewhere along the line, and most of the time you're not going to be disappointed.

Here's what I don't remember: writing that check so Allen Johnson could go to college. I think I've loaned and given money to other kids over the years, but I don't keep up with that. The truth is, Allen paid me far more than I paid him just by being a good student body president. I should have paid his whole tuition for four years.

But what is money? You like to have a little bit, but there are some things more important than others. The future education of young people is more important than money. We can find money. We can't continue denying kids the opportunities they should have because we don't have enough money. We're a rather rich country. What's more important—the lives of kids or money?

Chapter 57

౼

Ode to Secretaries, Custodians, and Team Managers

ANOTHER THING PEOPLE DON'T REALIZE is that schools are held together by three people: the secretary, the custodian, and the manager of the ball team. Those people are overlooked, but schools couldn't function without them. Who gets the glory when a school does well? The principal. The coach. But the secretary keeps the principal on track. Games don't get played without managers. School doors aren't opened and locked without the custodian. I wish I had realized that years ago.

So, with a lot of time to reflect, I began to realize how important all the people I associated with were important to my life. I realized there were a few people getting credit—principals, coaches, star athletes. And the people who were probably most important never got recognition. That included secretaries and custodians. I began to remember the value of those people to my life. So, as a symbol to all those people in that category, I began to think about the first custodian I worked with. His name was Josh Wright. He kept the Winyah schools and auditorium in Georgetown so clean. His wife helped him in the mornings before students came and his daughters helped him after they left. On top of all that, he'd build a coal fire to heat water for the football players. There wasn't a grate, so he'd do it on the concrete. That isn't easy to do. Josh worked hard for those schools for twenty-five years, and I never thanked him. He died in 1974.

I got so curious about Josh that I did some research on him. He and his wife had seven children, one of whom died in infancy. They sent all six of their living children to college. Now think about it: I was making $2,400 a year back then, and I was white with a college degree. He was probably making $1,000 a year. But I learned he was a trustee at Allen University and a member of the Theological Seminary Board of Trustees. And he was a very dedicated member at Bethel AME in Georgetown. Three times he was elected to the state AME church conference. All four of his daughters became public school teachers, and two stayed in Georgetown. One son became a dentist in Anchorage, Alaska, and the other went into business. If that doesn't say something good about Josh Wright, I don't know what does.

I decided I needed to do something about Josh Wright. He deserved some recognition. I called Nell Cribb, the very first secretary I ever worked with in Georgetown. Nell was really the secretary for the high school, but she also worked, unpaid, at the junior high school where I was principal. I also got in touch with Jay Bazemore, the very first football manager I ever worked with. We all called him "Jaybird," and I still do. The symbolism is important. Here I was going back to the beginning of my teaching career to honor my first custodian with the help of my first secretary and my first team manager—sixty years later! But what we were really doing, at least symbolically, was honoring the important but too often unnoticed good work of all custodians, secretaries, managers, and support staff and helpers of every kind. Lo and behold, Nell and Jaybird and I put our heads together and got it done, too. We decided to have a program to honor Josh and name some of the seats in the old Winyah auditorium after him and his family members. We got Doug Corkern, another one of my Georgetown students and ballplayers, to paint a portrait of Josh to hang in the auditorium. Doug is a retired architect in Bluffton and has been painting for years. The only photograph we could find of Josh for him to work from was the one Bethel AME used for his funeral bulletin. Jaybird wrote a summary of Josh's life to hang beside his portrait in the Winyah auditorium. My part was to challenge all those Winyah students to honor Josh by donating ten dollars for every time they appeared on stage. I bet they never thought about Josh cleaning up after their concerts and plays, and turning off the lights and locking the doors when they were over. Our goal was to restore all of the auditorium's three hundred seats for $350 each. I went ahead and sponsored eight seats in honor of Josh, his wife, Louise, and their children.

We had our program on a Saturday afternoon in September 2015. I was the emcee, and I was happy to see black and white people in the auditorium together. We had a white minister do the invocation and a black minister do the benediction. Jaybird and Doug made a few remarks about growing up in Georgetown and attending Winyah schools. Another one of my students, Joe Young—we called him "José" back then—sang "Amazing Grace." He's got a big baritone voice and he's white, of course. But then Della Prioleau, an African American lady with a beautiful voice, sang too. She's a member of Bethel AME. Josh's son, Dr. Joshua Wright Jr., came all the way from Alaska, and other members of the Wright family came too. Josh and Louise's grand-daughter, Rosalind Geathers, talked about how her grandparents asked her parents for one of their children to raise and keep them company in Georgetown, because all of their other children and grandchildren lived outside the state. Rosalind left New York City in 1969 and has been in Georgetown for fifty years, she said. She said she was "ecstatic" we were honoring her grandfather.

We unveiled Josh's portrait and the eight seats named for him and his family. And then best of all, before our refreshments, we all sang "The Battle Hymn of the Republic." I reminded them that when I was working at Winyah that song was forbidden. It was the first time that song was sung in that auditorium—and by a gathering of black and white people celebrating the contributions of a black man to his school and his community. "We're at 2015 now," I told them. I remember my exact words. "I think it's time that we sing lustily 'The Battle Hymn of the Republic' *together.*"

We had the words printed in the program, and Joe led us in the singing. We stood and sang together. That was the first time that song had ever been sung in the history of the Winyah auditorium. I was eighty-eight years old. I lived to see it, and I lived to sing it. "Our God is marching on," we sang. Our *truth* is marching on.

I think about these things a lot. And I talk about them too, when I speak to classes, during Dufford Diversity Week at Newberry College, to the former students that keep cycling back into my life, and at the many reunions and funerals I attend. When you've been in education as long as I have, you get invited to things that are happy and sad.

It's been a great life, it really has. I've got plenty of friends—all my students are still my kids. That will never change. If there's one thing

I've learned, it's important to talk with them. I did a lot of talking with kids, at school and at other places. I wasn't the first person at school. I have a great history of not being early. I was rarely there when the first bell rang. But I went to club meetings and ball games, anywhere my kids needed me to be for them. I was always the last person standing at night.

Epilogue

❧

Hold to the Past, Look to the Future

AÏDA ROGERS AND SALLEY MCINERNEY

O N ANY GIVEN DAY of the week, at about 10:00 A.M., you'll likely find William E. Dufford having a big breakfast at the Original Pancake House in a suburban shopping center in Columbia. For starters he has a small bowl of fruit, and then it's on to eggs and toast. The morning newspaper is spread out on his table. He sips his coffee and considers the day's tidings.

This summer morning, the man who most folks simply call "Dufford" also considers his legacy. What lessons he will leave behind, what lives he will have touched when he departs a world undoubtedly changed for the better by his presence in it.

"What I want people to know, what I want them to remember, is we need to continue to help out those who are left out or left behind."

He pushes a small slip of paper across the table. "This," he says, "is my ending message to the world. This is my legacy right here. This is what's important."

The paper proffers a quote from British philosopher Bertrand Russell: "One must care about a world one will not see."

"And this," Dufford says, pushing another piece of paper across the table, "is my commitment to the life I have lived. I found it years ago in a brochure published by the South Carolina Education Association."

It reads, "When the history of the world is written, the Greeks will be remembered for liberty, the Romans for law, the British for parliamentary government. But we in the United States will be remembered for one thing—the only nation in the history of the world to take seriously the idea of universal public education."

Public education.

Dufford has lived his life for its improvement. Specifically, for its equanimity and availability to all races. His legacy as a public educator who championed peaceful integration of schools across South Carolina during the 1960s and 1970s is a given.

But his impact runs deeper, into the lives of many people who have embraced his underdog philosophy—continuing to help out those who are left out or left behind.

Dennis Smith was president of the student body at Beaufort High School when Dufford arrived on the scene as the school's new principal in 1960.

Smith, who lives in Georgia now, described Beaufort High in 1960 as "a school on the brink of desegregation and one that seemed to have a distance that always existed between older teachers and younger students."

Dufford, Smith said, "took that channel of separation because of age and circumstance and built a bridge that the students had no fear of crossing because the landing spot on the other side was a friend and principal who had our best interests in mind."

Smith recalled Dufford's marching orders to him when the school year began.

"He immediately let me know that as student body president there were some extra duties he expected me to perform. He did not talk about setting examples, getting good grades, or any of that kind of stuff older people normally say. He told me that starting Monday, I would be delivering all the school announcements and he expected me to make certain he never had to worry about them being done. As the year progressed, I came to have total respect for him because it soon was apparent to all of us that if he told you something, you could put it in the bank. You could trust him. Every day he was in the hallways with his disarming smile and playful personality, greeting students—cajoling, challenging, pushing, helping.

"It was a thrill to walk down the aisle at graduation knowing that I had been given a very special gift. I had been given the gift of recognizing that if you care about and trust others, you end up with numerous blessings and wonderful memories. Bill Dufford gave that to me."

As an adult, Smith went on to care about and trust others as well. He became the chief operating officer of one of the largest food banks in the United States. And he guided a lot of young people along the way.

"Now that I am retired and nearing the midpoint of my seventies, I look back and count the number of young people I had a chance to trust, a chance to tell them that this is your responsibility."

"I was fortunate enough," Smith said, "to have fulfilled Bill's legacy."

That legacy now continues through younger generations. Smith recently sent his grandson Avery, a student at the University of Florida, to see Dufford. Avery had come to Columbia as one of Florida's student ambassadors when the Gators played the Gamecocks, but he also made a point of spending the afternoon visiting with his grandfather's mentor.

These bridges between the past and the future have become common in Dufford's life. Lawton Swann, son of Dufford's former student and longtime colleague Reed Swann, stayed with Dufford while earning his master's degree in education at the University of South Carolina. Continuing the "family business," Lawton now works in Lexington County's District 1 as a technology integration specialist.

Twenty-something Luke Morris, a graduate of the College of Charleston and the son of sports columnist Ron Morris, a friend of Bill Dufford's, has known Dufford most of his life. Luke's experience is also indicative of the multi-generational connections Dufford has fostered.

"I first met Bill when I was around ten or eleven years old, through my father. Bill was a guest at our house for a few Thanksgiving dinners throughout my years in middle and high school. These dinners were when I really got to know who Bill was and what he had done during integration.

"One thing that always struck me was how he included everyone in any discussion or activity. Even though I was a teenager, he always asked me how I felt about topics, including politics and current events, even though everyone at the table was certainly more knowledgeable than I was. Not only did he include me, he also seemed genuinely interested in what I had to say and any story I had to tell."

When Luke finished his freshman year of college, he worked with Dufford, helping the educator organize a lifetime's worth of collected written material—correspondence, files, and photos.

"Looking through his files, photos, and books gave me a view into the incredible life he has lived and the incredible work he has done. As a still naive eighteen-year-old, digging deep into Dufford's life showed me that [integration] wasn't natural but rather a hard-fought battle that lasted much longer than it should have.

"I have always held Dufford in high regard since I first met him, but since I was given the opportunity to spend that summer with him, he is not only a role model, but he also influences how I go about my life now. Dufford has never seen anyone as above or beneath another person, whether they are rich, poor, black, or white, and this is something that I strive to live up to as I live my life every day."

While many of these generation-spanning relationships grew out of Bill Dufford's forty years in public education, some even predate that.

As a Newberry College student, Dufford, along with a fellow student, coached the junior high school varsity basketball team in Newberry. Among the players that year was Phil Spotts, who later became a successful teacher and coach in Newberry himself. When Phil's son Langston needed a place to stay while attending USC in Columbia, Dufford welcomed him. Lang earned his bachelor's and master's degrees and now works in medical administration. To this day, Bill Dufford is a welcomed member of the extended Spotts family, all thanks to a mentoring connection he made while still a college student himself.

Through these lifelong friendships with his former students and their families, children, and now grandchildren—like Dennis and Avery Smith, Reed and Lawton Swann, Ron and Luke Morris. Phil and Lang Spotts—Dufford has been able to hold to the past while also looking to the future, a brighter, more inclusive future his career in public education has helped shape through all the lives he has impacted.

As for Dufford himself, he finishes his breakfast on this summer morning and has a kind word for the waitress, who has stopped by the table with a check. He folds his napkin and pushes it underneath the edge of the empty plate.

His has been a long, good, and productive life. He is humbled by the people who have been a part of it—a life, he says, with which he is satisfied.

"I couldn't have been more fortunate. Many people were there to help me along the way. They were kind and they were generous. I guess I started working with kids in 1949. Yep, that would be about right. And I'm still working with them. They keep me young. They think I helped them, and in fact they helped me."

Dufford takes a last sip of coffee.

"Here's the thing," he says, getting ready to leave, gathering up his newspaper. "None of my life was planned. I was just always asked to do this or that. Things just fell into my lap. There was never any formalized plan, just forward progress."

Forward progress indeed. With that, Bill Dufford continues to look to the possibilities he sees in his students, their children, grandchildren, and generations to come, and he continues to motivate and inspire others to bring people together as best they can, leaving no one out, welcoming everyone along toward that bright unrealized future.

∽

Deep and wide—that's one way to describe Bill Dufford's influence in South Carolina. During his forty years in public education and into retirement, colleagues and students learned from him before launching or continuing their own remarkable careers. Here's a look at what happened to some of the "characters" in the Bill Dufford story:

Leighton Cubbage earned a full football scholarship to Clemson University, where he played linebacker and graduated in political science in 1977. In 1989 he cofounded a telecommunications company that made $100 million in revenue by 1995. Running a successful business led him to accounting courses at Greenville Technical College, to which he later donated money for a child development center named for his mother. Involved in real estate, banking, car dealerships, and telecommunications, Cubbage was chair of the Greenville Hospital System for two terms. In 2014 he became chair of the South Carolina Venture Capital Authority. Having also studied business at the University of North Carolina at Chapel Hill, Cubbage lives in Greenville, where he tries to practice the positive, hands-on, "transformational leadership" he learned from Bill Dufford.

Dr. Dill Gamble earned his Ed.D. in education administration from the University of South Carolina in 1985 and spent the next ten years as superintendent of schools in Allendale County. In 1995 he returned to his first love, history, and became a history professor at Voorhees College in Denmark, where he also chaired the Department of Social Sciences. He retired in 2003 and lives in Columbia.

Inspired by Governor Dick Riley, Richard Gergel came back to Columbia in 1979, having just graduated from Duke University Law School. After practicing for almost thirty years, he was appointed as a U.S. District Court judge in 2010, following his nomination by President Barack Obama the previous year. In 2014, Judge Gergel made headlines—and history—with his ruling that South Carolina's ban on same-sex marriage was unconstitutional.

Baseball player Allen Johnson was named All South, All Region, and All American in 1971 and 1972 at Wingate College, where he pitched for seventeen wins and four losses. On full scholarship at USC in 1973 and 1974, he pitched eighty-eight innings and earned two letters, making twenty-nine appearances. He earned an associate's degree from Wingate, where he's in the athletics hall of fame, and a bachelor of science in physical education and health from USC. Johnson was drafted in the twenty-fifth round by the Detroit Tigers and played for two years before an injury led him to scout for the team. He later earned a master's in sports administration from the U.S. Sports Academy and worked for Sumter District 17 as a teacher and coach. Almost every younger member of Johnson's extended family graduated from college, a fact he attributes directly to Bill Dufford. "It's been wonderful for me simply because someone cared," he says. His wife, Ann, is a math teacher.

Dr. Burnett Joiner has been president of two colleges—LeMoyne-Owen in Memphis and Livingstone and Hood Theological Seminary in Salisbury, North Carolina. An educational consultant for more than two hundred school districts and institutions in the United States and the Caribbean, Joiner has appeared as a guest expert on education matters on radio and television, including *Learning in America*, the PBS MacNeil/Lehrer special. In 1990, the Association of Teacher Educators recognized him as one of America's top leaders in education. Listed in *Who's Who Among Black Americans*, Joiner is dean of the School of Continuing Education at Benedict College in Columbia.

Potential high school dropout Walter McRackan graduated magna cum laude from Duke University in 1975. He also attended the London School of Economics and the University of London. While getting his master's degree in real estate and property finance from the University of South Carolina, McRackan rented from Bill Dufford. It was Dufford who drove him to Antioch College in Ohio when his parents' car broke down in the summer of 1972. Now living and working in Charleston, McRackan travels the world in his free time. He has been to at least sixty countries.

Dr. Moses Rabb earned his Ph.D. in counseling education from the University of South Carolina in 1981. After leaving the Center for Integrated Education, he worked as the director of training and director of treatment at the South Carolina Commission on Alcohol and Drug Abuse. He also started two companies.

After leaving Sumter High School in 1971, Steve Satterfield coached at Clemson University and Wofford College. He remembers 1969 as the most exciting year of his life, and points to Bill Dufford's leadership as the reason why. "He released me from becoming a fair teacher to becoming a great teacher. If he goes out as principal somewhere, I'm going to be the head football coach," he promises. Satterfield lives in Spartanburg County, where he reads and writes poetry, exercises daily, and mentors troubled people.

Pastor Dermon Sox Sr. preached at St. John's Lutheran Church in Beaufort until 1970. He retired in 1971, finishing his ministry at

Bethany and Nazareth Lutheran churches in Lexington County. He died in 1994 in Edmund, a quarter-mile from where his father's log cabin once stood.

Besides serving on race matters with the South Carolina Synod, Pastor Dermon Sox Jr. served at the national level as a member of the Consulting Committee on Minority Group Interest of the Lutheran Church in America. He also served on the ecumenical level as a member of the Racial Justice Committee of the interdenominational Christian Action Council in 1993 and 1994. Sox retired in 1996 and teaches Sunday school occasionally at Christus Victor Lutheran Church in Columbia. His daughter, Diana Sox Edis, is vicar at St. Paul's Lutheran Church in Prince Rupert, British Columbia, focusing on multiculturalism and serving the Haida people of the Pacific Northwest.

Reed Swann continued his legacy of fair integration at Barnwell High School. After retiring in 1989, he ran for the Barnwell District 45 school board, serving twelve years. He also served on numerous statewide education groups, and in 2002 he was elected president of the South Carolina School Boards Association. Having given up broadcasting, Swann took up community theater, appearing in major roles in *The Music Man*, *Camelot*, *Carousel*, and *Inherit the Wind*.

Dr. J. Earl Vaughn retired from Sumter 17 in 1991, having served thirty-three years in the district as a teacher, principal, and assistant superintendent for administration. A veteran of the U.S. Air Force, Vaughn earned a bachelor's degree from Morris College, a master's degree from South Carolina State College, an Ed.S. from the University of South Carolina, and an Ed.D. from the University of Tennessee. He died in 2013 at the age of eighty-one, leaving his wife, DeLores, and their son, Gregory, a medical doctor.

Eight years after enrolling, Tim Conroy graduated from USC in 1983. He later earned two master's degrees, from the Citadel and Cambridge College. He worked for twenty-eight years in education, mainly as a special education teacher across the state and for the South Carolina Autism Society. On June 7, 1986, Conroy married Terrye McKenzie at Rutledge Chapel on the USC campus. Bill Dufford was his best man.

Pat Conroy was an internationally known best-selling author whose novels, including *The Prince of Tides*, *The Great Santini*, and *The Lords of Discipline*, have been adapted into popular films. He wrote about his principal in *The Water Is Wide* and "The Bill Dufford Summer," a chapter in *The Pat Conroy Cookbook*. Conroy's foreword to this book was originally delivered as his introduction for Bill Dufford at the 2014 South Carolina Governor's Awards in the Humanities luncheon and also appeared as a chapter in *A Lowcountry Heart: Reflections on a Writing Life*, published in October 2016 following Conroy's death from pancreatic cancer on March 4, 2016.

In 2014, Bill Dufford received the prestigious Governor's Award in the Humanities from the Humanities Council[SC], and in 2015 the equally prestigious South Carolina Order of the Palmetto, South Carolina's highest civilian honor. In attendance at the Governor's Award event, in addition to Pat Conroy, were several of Dufford's former colleagues and students, including Richard Gergel, Allen Johnson, Burnett Joiner, Hayes Mizell, Reed Swann, Moses Rabb, and Steve Satterfield. The Order of the Palmetto was presented by Representative James Smith at the Newberry Opera House, also with Conroy in attendance. Among the many people who wrote letters of support for the honor was Hayes Mizell. "Educators and youth who once doubted their abilities to rise to the demands of professional and personal challenges achieved success because of Dr. Dufford's active belief in their potential, and his support and encouragement," he wrote. "Particularly during the uncertainty and tension that characterized the desegregation of South Carolina's public schools, Dr. Dufford provided effective leadership at both local and state levels. He guided educators and students to take responsibility for anticipating and preventing structural and social problems that plagued many schools. In doing so, he demonstrated how school leaders could not only manage desegregation, but foster integration characterized by respect and fairness for all participants."

By mid-September of 2015, about one hundred of the three hundred seats of Georgetown's Winyah auditorium's restored downstairs had been sponsored for $350 each, with former students given the opportunity to have their names and the years they were in school noted on them. Bill Dufford sponsored eight of the seats, one for Josh Wright, his wife, Louise, and the six children who survived them. In this commitment to honor Wright, his first custodian, with the help of Nell Cribb, his first school secretary, and Jay "Jaybird" Bazemore, his first team manager, Dufford is still working with vigor and determination to see that everyone is recognized and no one is overlooked. This is his instructive legacy of inclusion that has defined his long career in public education and which continues even now into the twilight of his life.

In October 2016, Newberry College history professor and archivist Tracy Power unearthed a letter in Bill Dufford's collected papers, dated 1968 and unseen since 1970. The correspondence from the late Pat Conroy to his high school principal read like a voice from beyond the grave, not only affirming the importance to Conroy of his Beaufort High School experience in fostering his interests in both teaching and writing, but also serving as a testimony of the incredible power one educator can have in shaping the life of a student. That, as Conroy writes here, is immortality.

Dear Doc,

The kid you once shoved around the St. Paul locker room for ten minutes has managed to live down his nefarious past or meager beginnings. He is now cruising on the Aegean Sea having just left Crete, en route to Beirut Lebanon. I've been doing a lot of thinking on this cruise, and it seems whenever I think you loom as an important figure, presiding over and in some unfathomable way, guiding and directing whatever decision I make. So it has been for five years. So it is now. For three years now I have wondered about my position in the great scheme of things. This year it became almost agony. The thought of gradual deterioration, of age, of death, of everything significant to man during his tenure on earth. I have met three interesting people on the journey. They are intelligent—older—and they are still asking the same questions I am now asking myself. I don't know if I ever will be content with what I am doing, but I wonder now if anything but the human oxen of the world ever are. Everything I have done since leaving Beaufort has been a reflection of the summer I spent with you digging those damn ditches and painting those damn bookcases. I have never understood the dynamics of hero worship—maybe it was the discovery of the father I never had as a youth and finally found in you, a father that was not only stern but was tender, a father of both the storm and the sun. All these things come before me now, Doc, all these things in a mixture of joy and sorrow—the realization of days lost, memories vanished, delicious moments carried and discarded by divergent winds. It is important for you to know this effect you have had and I believe you know it but in the shortness and horrible brevity of life I want to get everything said—everything. Someday I will exert the same influence over someone, and I want him to tell me. This is immortality. For what I have learned from you I will pass on, and it will be passed on and passed on. I was in New York before I left for

Europe and walked over to the Hotel Chesterfield from Radio City Music Hall. Nothing had changed much. Except the years and the memories. This time I smiled.

Pat